# THE KREG[EL]
# PICTORIAL GU[IDE]

# BIBLE FACTS
# & FIGURES

## TIM DOWLEY

## Contents

**Kregel**
*Publications*

# Some Ways into Your Bible

## Some fascinating Bible statistics

| | Old Testament | New Testament |
|---|---|---|
| Number of books | 39 | 27 |
| Number of chapters | 929 | 260 |
| Number of verses | 23,214 | 7,959 |
| Number of words | 592,493 | 181,253 |
| Longest book | Psalms | Luke |
| Shortest book | Obadiah | 3 John |
| Longest chapter | Psalm 119 | Matthew 26 |
| Shortest chapter | Psalm 117 | Revelation 15 |
| Longest verse | Esther 8:9 | Revelation 20:4 |
| Shortest verse | 1 Chronicles | John 11:35 ("Jesus wept.") |
| Middle book | Proverbs | 2 Thessalonians |
| Middle chapter | Job 29 | Romans 13–14 |
| Middle verse | 2 Chronicles 20:13 | Acts 7:7 |

**Total number of verses in both Testaments:** 31,173.

**Middle chapter of the Bible:** Psalm 117

**Middle verse:** Psalm 118:5

**Most mentioned character:** David (1,118 times)

**Longest word:** Mahershalalhashbaz (Isaiah 8:1)

NB *These figures are based on English Bibles and may vary according to the translation.*

### Bible translation facts
• More than 6,500 languages are spoken in the world.
• Of these, 2,167 languages have some or all of the Bible (355 complete Bibles, 850 New Testaments).
• About 4,333 languages are still without any part of the Bible.

The smallest Bible ever published was the Mite Bible published by Oxford University Press in 1896. Its pages were 28 x 41 mm (1.62 x 1.12 in.), it was 900 pages long and 13 mm (0.5 in.) thick.

## A Bible Reading Plan

*If you would like to read the Bible systematically and carefully, the following reading order will be helpful. Although this plan does not include every book of the Bible, it will give you a good overview of Scripture if followed regularly.*

**New Testament**
1. Mark
2. John
3. Luke–Acts
4. 1 Thessalonians
5. 1 Corinthians
6. Romans
7. Philemon
8. Philippians
9. Ephesians
10. 2 Timothy
11. 1 Peter
12. 1 John
13. Revelation (chapters 1–5 and 19:6–22:21)

**Old Testament**
14. Genesis
15. Exodus (chapters 1–24)
16. Numbers (10:11–21:35)
17. Deuteronomy (chapters 1–11)
18. Joshua (chapters 1–12 and 22–24)
19. Judges (sample)
20. 1–2 Samuel (sample)
21. 1–2 Kings (sample)
22. Nehemiah
23. Amos
24. Isaiah (chapters 1–12)
25. Jeremiah (chapters 1–25 and 30–33)
26. Isaiah (chapters 40–55)
27. Ruth
28. Jonah
29. Psalms (some examples of the major types)
30. Job (perhaps 1–14 and 38–42)
31. Proverbs (chapters 1–9)
32. Daniel (chapters 1–6; sample chapters 7–12)

## Noah's Boat

**The boat God told Noah to build** (133 meters x 22.2 meters x 13.4 meters [roughly 436 ft. x 73 ft. x 44 ft.]) was big enough to hold 432 double-decker buses. There was plenty of room for the 35,000 or so animals that were saved from the flood with Noah and his family.

## BIBLE VERSES FOR SPECIAL OCCASIONS

### Birthdays
*Joshua 1:1-9; Psalms 1; 23; 25; 37:3-7; 39:1-7; 90; 91; 139; Proverbs 3:5-8; 26:3-4; 41:10; 43:1-3; 46:4; Lamentations 3:22-26; Luke 1:46-55; John 6:35; 8:12; 10:1-30; Romans 8:28-39; 11:33-36; Ephesians 1:3-14; Philippians 4:4-7; Hebrews 10:23; 1 John 1:7-9.*

### Baptism, dedication of children and confirmation
*Joshua 1:5-9; 1 Samuel 1:27-28; Psalms 1; 23; 111; 121; Ecclesiastes 12:1; Matthew 3:11-17; 10:32-33; 28:18-20; Mark 10:13-16; John 3:1-21; 15:1-17; Acts 8:36-40; 16:30-33; 22:16; Romans 6:1-14; 1 Corinthians 12:12-13; Galatians 3:26-28; Ephesians 3:14-21,4:1-6; Philippians 1:1-11; Colossians 2:6-14; 1 Timothy 6:11-16; Titus 3:4-7; 1 Peter 3:18-22; Jude 24.*

### Thanksgiving
*Deuteronomy 6:10-19; 8; Psalm 33; 65; 95; 100; 103; 104; 107; 111; 116, 126; 136; 145; 147; Isaiah 12; Luke 12:13-34; Acts 14:17; 1 Corinthians 3:5-9; Colossians 2:16-17; Hebrews 13:15-16; Revelation 5.*

### Wedding day
*Genesis 2:18-25; Ruth 1:16-17; Psalms 67; 84; 100; 118:24-29; 121; 127; 128; 139; Matthew 19:4-6; John 2:1-11; 1 Corinthians 13; Ephesians 5:22-33; Colossians 3:12-21.*

### Retirement
*Joshua 1:7-9; 1 Samuel 7:12; Psalm 23; 71:14-24; Isaiah 43:18-21; 46:4; John 14:27; 1 Corinthians 1:8; Philippians 3:7-16*

## CHRISTMAS AND NEW YEAR READING PLAN

**December 20:** *Luke 1:26-38*
**Jesus' birth foretold**

**December 21:** *Luke 1:39-56*
**Mary and Elizabeth**

**December 22:** *Luke 1:67-80*
**Zechariah's song**

**December 23:** *Colossians 1:15-20*
**Who Jesus is**

**December 24:** *John 1:1-18*
**The Word became flesh**

**Christmas Day:** *Luke 2:1-7*
**The Saviour is born**

**December 26:** *Luke 2:8-20*
**The shepherds and the angels**

**December 27:** *Matthew 2:1-12*
**The Magi worship Jesus**

**December 28:** *Luke 2:21-32*
**Jesus is presented in the Temple**

**December 29:** *Luke 2:36-38*
**The redemption of Jerusalem**

**December 30:** *Matthew 2:13-18*
**Jesus is kept safe**

**December 31:** *Psalm 90*
**Teach us to number our days**

**New Year's Day:** *Exodus 33:7-23*
**Show me your glory**

**January 2:** *Philippians 3:7-14*
**Pressing on to the goal**

**January 3:** *Joshua 1:1-9*
**Be strong and courageous**

**January 4:** *Matthew 6:25-34*
**Do not worry**

**January 5:** *Romans 8:28-39*
**More than conquerors**

**January 6:** *Philippians 4:4-9*
**Rejoice in the Lord**

## EASTER READING PLAN

**Palm Sunday:** *Luke 19:28-44*
**The approach to Jerusalem**

**Monday:** *Luke 19:45-48*
**Jesus at the Temple**

**Tuesday:** *Philippians 2:5-11*
**Obedient to death**

**Wednesday:** *1 Peter 2:21-25*
**Christ suffered for you**

**Maundy Thursday:** Luke *22:7-71;* John 17
**The last supper; Jesus' arrest**

**Good Friday:** *Luke 23; Isaiah 53*
**The crucifixion**

**Saturday:** *Matthew 27:62-66*
**The guard at the tomb**

**Easter Day:** *Matthew 28:1-15*
**The resurrection**

**Easter Monday:** *John 20:24-31*
**My Lord and my God!**

**Tuesday:** *1 Corinthians 15:12-58*
**Victory over death**

**Wednesday:** *Acts 2:22-41*
**Why Jesus died**

**Thursday:** *Romans 1:1-7*
**Jesus Christ our Lord**

**Friday:** *Romans 6:5-14*
**United with him**

**Saturday:** *Colossians 3:1-4*
**Raised with Christ**

**Sunday:** *Revelation 1:4-18*
**Alive for ever and ever**

**Ascension Day**
*Luke 24:50-53; Acts 1:1-11*

**Pentecost** (Whitsun) *Acts1:8; 2:1-2; 19:1-7 Ephesians 4:30.*

---

*If you want to have an idea of what's in the Apocrypha, here is a suggested reading plan.*

**Apocrypha**
1. Tobit
2. Ecclesiasticus (sample chapters 1–23)
3. 1 Maccabees (1:1–9:22) or 2 Maccabees
4. Judith
5. The Wisdom of Solomon (chapters 1–9)
6. 2 Esdras (chapters 3–14)

# When You Are in Need . . .

## Bible Verses to Look At When You Need Help

The Bible includes many promises that can help and encourage us in times of sadness, difficulty or stress. Here are some verses that show us God's help. Read and meditate over them:

**• When you feel afraid**
"I sought the LORD, and he answered me; he delivered me from all my fears" *Psalm 34:4.*
*See also Psalms 27; 46; 56; 91; Matthew 8:23–27.*

**• When you feel alone**
"So do not fear, for I am with you; do not be dismayed, for I am your God" *Isaiah 41:10.*
*See also Psalms 23; 73:23–24; Isaiah 49:14–16; John 14:15–21.*

**• When you are anxious or worried**
"Cast all your anxiety on him because he cares for you" *1 Peter 5:7.*
*See also Isaiah 43:1–13; Matthew 6:25–34; 11:28; Philippians 4:4–7.*

**• When you have been bereaved**
"Blessed are those who mourn, for they will be comforted" *Matthew 5:4.*
*See also Psalm 23; John 11:21–27; 1 Corinthians 15:51–57; 1 Thessalonians 4:13–18; Revelation 21:1–5.*

**• When you feel discouraged**
"Why are you downcast, O my soul? Why so disturbed within me? Put your hope in God" *Psalm 42:5.*
*See also Psalms 34:18; 40:1–3; Lamentations 3:20–23; Romans 8:28–39; 2 Corinthians 4:7–18.*

**• When you have doubts**
"I do believe; help me overcome my unbelief!" *Mark 9:24.*
*See also Isaiah 40:27–31; Matthew 11:1–6; John 20:19–29; Acts 17:22–28.*

**• When you feel you have done wrong**
"But God demonstrates his own love for us in this: While we were still sinners, Christ died for us" *Romans 5:8.*
*See also Psalm 51; Luke 15:11–24.*

**• When you feel distant from God**
"Come near to God and he will come near to you" *James 4:8.*
*See also Psalm 139:1–18; John 10:29; Acts 17:24–31.*

**• When you are ill or in pain**
"My grace is sufficient for you, for my power is made perfect in weakness" *2 Corinthians 12:9.*
*See also Psalm 103:1–4; Romans 8:18–25; 2 Corinthians 4:16–18.*

**• When you need peace**
"You will keep in perfect peace him whose mind is steadfast, because he trusts in you" *Isaiah 26:3.*
*See also John 14:27; Romans 5:1–5; Philippians 4:4–7.*

**• When you are tempted**
"We have one [a High Priest] who has been tempted in every way, just as we are—yet was without sin" *Hebrews 4:15.*
*See also Luke 4:1–13; Ephesians 6:10–20; James 1:2–6, 12–18; 4:7–8; 1 Peter 5:8–9.*

**• When you are tired or weak**
"Come to me, all you who are weary and burdened, and I will give you rest. Take my yoke upon you and learn from me, for I am gentle and humble in heart, and you will find rest for your souls" *Matthew 11:28–29.*
*See also Joshua 1:5–9; Isaiah 40:28–31; 2 Corinthians 4:16–18; 12:9–10; Philippians 4:12–13.*

**• When you need guidance**
"In all your ways acknowledge him, and he will make your paths straight" *Proverbs 3:6.*
*See also Psalm 48:14; John 14:16; 16:13.*

## Model Prayers of the Bible

| | |
|---|---|
| **Complaint** | *Numbers 14:13–19* |
| **Confession** | *Psalm 32; Psalm 51; Ezra 9:5–15* |
| **Dedication** | *2 Chronicles 6:14–42* |
| **Dependence** | *2 Chronicles 20:6–12* |
| **Despair** | *Psalm 73* |
| **For believers** | *Ephesians 1:16–23; Ephesians 3:15–21* |
| **For blessing** | *Psalm 90* |
| **For deliverance** | *Isaiah 37:14–20* |
| **For healing** | *Isaiah 38:3,9–20* |
| **For restoration** | *Daniel 9:4–19* |
| **For unity** | *John 17* |
| **In national crisis** | *2 Kings 19:14–19* |
| **Intercession** | *Genesis 18:16–33; Exodus 32:11–13* |
| **Petition** | *Acts 4:24–30* |
| **Praise** | *Luke 1:46–55* |
| **Recommitment** | *John 2:2–9* |
| **Thanksgiving** | *1 Samuel 2:1–10; Psalms 16; 65* |
| **The Lord's Prayer** | *Matthew 6:9–13; Luke 11:2–4* |
| **Trust** | *Psalm 23* |

## Some well-known Bible passages

| | |
|---|---|
| **The creation story** | *Genesis 1:1–2:7* |
| **The fall** | *Genesis 3:1-24* |
| **The flood** | *Genesis 6:1–9:17* |
| **The call of Abraham** | *Genesis 12:1-9* |
| **The Ten Commandments** | *Exodus 20:1-17* |
| **The shepherd's psalm** | *Psalm 23* |
| **The birth of Jesus** | *Matthew 1:18–2:23; Luke 1:26–2:40* |
| **The golden rule** | *Luke 6:31* |
| **The Sermon on the Mount** | *Matthew 5–7* |
| **The Beatitudes** | *Matthew 5:3-11* |
| **The Lord's Prayer** | *Luke 11:2-4* |
| **The prodigal son** | *Luke 15:11-32* |
| **The good Samaritan** | *Luke 10:29-37* |
| **The last supper** | *Matthew 26:17-30; Mark 14:12-26* |
| **The death of Christ** | *Luke 23:26-56; John 19:16-42* |
| **The resurrection of Christ** | *Matthew 28; Luke 24; John 20* |
| **The ascension of Christ** | *Acts 1:1-12* |
| **The coming of the Holy Spirit** | *Acts 2:1-21* |
| **The conversion of Paul** | *Acts 9:1-31* |
| **The love chapter** | *1 Corinthians 13* |
| **The faith chapter** | *Hebrews 11* |

# Where to find help in the book of Psalms

## Psalms to read when you're feeling:

**Afraid** *3, 13, 27, 46, 56, 59, 64, 91, 118, 121*
**Alone** *9, 12, 13, 27, 40, 43*
**Angry** *17, 28, 36, 37, 109*
**Burned out** *6, 63*
**Cheated** *41*
**Confused** *10, 12, 73*
**Depressed** *27, 34, 42, 43, 88, 143*
**Disappointed** *16, 92, 102, 130*
**Distressed** *13, 25, 31, 40, 107*
**Guilty** *19, 32, 38, 51*
**Impatient** *4, 13, 27, 37, 40, 89, 123*
**Insecure** *3, 5, 12, 91*
**Insignificant** *8, 23, 86, 90, 139*
**Insulted** *41, 70*
**Jealous** *37, 73*
**Joyful** *96, 149*
**Like giving up** *29, 43, 145*
**Lost** *23, 139*
**Overwhelmed** *25, 69, 142*
**Proud** *14, 30, 49*
**Purposeless** *25, 39, 90*
**Self-confident** *24*
**Sorry/repentant** *51, 66*
**Stressed** *12, 31, 34, 43, 56, 62, 84*
**Thankful** *30, 33, 66, 96, 103, 104, 113, 118, 136, 138*
**Threatened** *143, 144*
**Trapped** *7, 17, 42, 88, 142*
**Vengeful** *3, 109*
**Weak** *13, 18, 23, 28, 29, 62, 70, 86, 102*
**Worried** *37*
**Worshipful** *19, 29, 148, 150*

## Psalms to read when you're facing:

**Competition** *113*
**Criticism** *35, 56, 120*
**Danger** *11*
**Death** *23*
**Decisions** *1, 25, 62, 119*
**Discouragement** *12, 42, 55, 86, 107, 142*
**Discrimination** *94*
**Doubts** *34, 37*
**Enemies** *3, 25, 35, 41, 56, 59*
**Evil people** *10, 36, 49, 52, 109*
**Hypocrisy** *26, 50*
**Injustice** *7, 9, 10, 17, 56, 94*
**Insults** *35, 43*
**Lies** *5, 12, 120*
**Old age** *71, 92*
**Persecution** *1, 3, 7*
**Poverty** *12, 34, 146*
**Punishment** *6, 38, 39*
**Sickness** *6, 22, 23, 41, 116, 139*
**Slaughter** *46, 83*
**Sorrow/grief** *6, 23, 31, 71, 77, 94, 123*
**Success** *18, 112, 126, 128*
**Temptation** *38, 141*
**Troubles** *34, 55, 86, 102, 142, 145*
**Verbal cruelty** *35, 120*

## Psalms to read when you want:

**Acceptance** *139*
**Answers** *4, 17, 119*
**Confidence** *46, 71*
**Courage** *11, 27*
**Fellowship with God** *5, 16, 25, 37*
**Forgiveness** *32, 38, 40, 51, 86, 103*
**Friendship** *16*
**Godliness** *15, 25*
**Guidance/direction** *1, 19, 32, 37, 89, 146*

**Healing** *6, 41, 103*
**Hope** *16, 17, 18, 23, 27*
**Humility** *19, 131, 147*
**Illumination** *19*
**Integrity** *24, 25*
**Joy** *9, 16, 33, 47, 84, 96, 97, 98, 100*
**Justice** *2, 7, 14, 26, 37, 82*
**Knowledge of God** *18, 19, 29, 65, 89, 97, 103, 145, 147*
**Leadership** *72*
**Miracles** *60, 111*
**Money** *15, 16, 49*
**Peace** *3, 4, 85*
**Perspective** *2, 11, 73*
**Prayer** *5, 17, 27, 61*
**Protection** *7, 16, 18, 23, 27, 31, 91, 125*
**Provision** *34, 81*
**Reassurance** *15, 23, 26, 112, 121*
**Rest** *23, 27*
**Salvation** *103, 146*
**Security** *34, 84, 91*
**Vindication** *9, 35, 109*
**Wisdom** *1, 16, 19, 64, 111*

# From Abraham to the Exodus

## What are the main events in the life of Abraham?

| | Genesis reference | New Testament comment | Abraham's age |
|---|---|---|---|
| Abram is born | 11:26 | | |
| Called by God | 12:1-3 | Hebrews 11:8 | |
| Enters into Canaan | 12:4-9 | Acts 7:2-8 | 75 |
| Abram and Lot separate | 13:1-18 | | |
| Abram rescues Lot | 14:1-17 | | |
| Abram is blessed by Melchizedek | 14:18-24 | Hebrews 7:1-10 | |
| God's covenant with Abram: his faith is reckoned to him as righteousness | 15:1-21 | Romans 4:1-17 Galatians 3:6-25 Hebrews 6:13-20 | 85 |
| Abraham fathers Ishmael by Hagar | 16:1-16 | | 86 |
| Abraham is circumcised and promised a son by Sarah | 17:1-27 | Romans 4:18-25 Hebrews 11:11, 12 | 99 |
| Abraham pleads for Sodom | 18:20-33 | | |
| Sodom destroyed, Lot saved | 19:1-38 | | |
| Isaac is born | 21:1-7 | | 100 |
| Abraham sends Hagar and Ishmael away | 21:8-21 | Galatians 4:21-31 | 103 |
| Abraham is challenged to sacrifice Isaac | 22:1-19 | Hebrews 11:17-19 James 2:20-24 | |
| Sarah dies and is buried at Hebron | 23:1-20 | | 137 |
| Abraham sends for bride for Isaac – Rebecca | 24:1-67 | | 140 |
| Abraham dies | 25:1-11 | | 175 |

## What were the ten plagues of Egypt?

**Exodus 7–12**

**Moses warned Pharaoh of ten plagues on the land of Egypt. Since the Egyptian gods were thought to be bound up with the forces of nature, each disaster was an attack on their power.**

**1. Water to blood** *Exodus 7:14-24*
The Nile turned to blood. Possibly red dirt or algae clogged the Nile and killed the fish, making the river the Egyptians regarded as the source of life smell of death. The first six plagues all seem to emerge from the Nile and demonstrate God's power over it.

**2. Frogs** *Exodus 8:1-15*
Frogs overran the land and when they died, polluted Egypt.

**3. Gnats** *Exodus 8:16-19*
A small stinging insect, such as the sand flea, is probably meant. Egypt's magicians could not repeat this miracle and told Pharaoh it was the work of God.

**4. Flies** *Exodus 8:20-32*
Swarms, possibly of biting swamp flies, infested Egypt. The diseases they bear may have been the source of the fifth and sixth plagues.

**5. Death of cattle** *Exodus 9:1-7*
Many believe that the plague that struck the cattle of Egypt was anthrax. The Israelite cattle were immune, showing that God distinguished between his people and their oppressors.

**6. Boils** *Exodus 9:8-12*
Probably skin anthrax, carried by the bites of the flies, which fed on the rotting frogs.

**7. Hail** *Exodus 9:13-35*
The storm ruined the barley and flax, but spared the land of Goshen, occupied by the Israelites.

**8. Locusts** *Exodus 10:1-20*
Locusts stripped the land of any remaining crops. Following the other plagues that devastated the economy of Egypt, this plague was disastrous.

**9. Darkness** *Exodus 10:21-29*
The sun, representing the Egyptian god Ka, was darkened for three days. Some suggest this was due to a khamsin, a fierce wind that fills the air with dirt. The text, however, indicates a deeper and more terrifying darkness.

**10. Death of the firstborn**
*Exodus 11:1–12:36*
This final plague took the firstborn of every Egyptian household, but left the Israelites untouched. This caused such terror that Pharaoh finally urged Moses to lead Israel out of his land to freedom. The gods of Egypt were shown to be powerless before the God of the Hebrews.

# Abraham's family tree

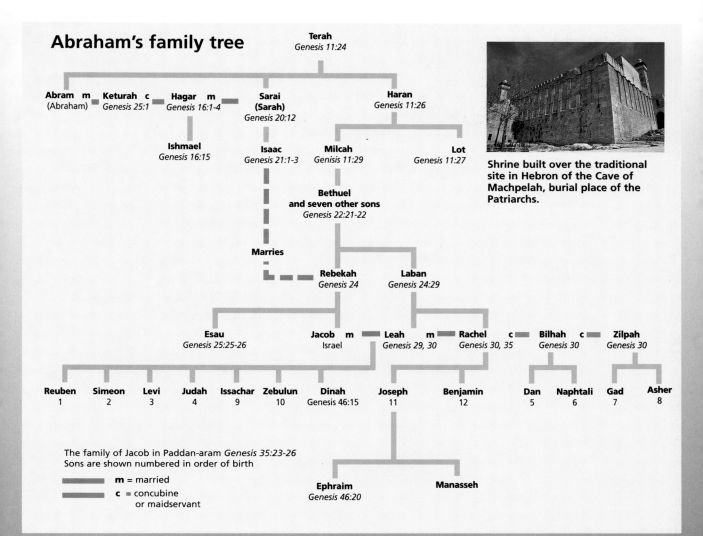

**Terah**
*Genesis 11:24*

**Abram** m ▬ **Keturah** c ▬ **Hagar** m ▬ **Sarai (Sarah)** *Genesis 20:12*    **Haran** *Genesis 11:26*
(Abraham)    *Genesis 25:1*    *Genesis 16:1-4*

**Ishmael** *Genesis 16:15*    **Isaac** *Genesis 21:1-3*    **Milcah** *Genisis 11:29*    **Lot** *Genesis 11:27*

**Bethuel and seven other sons** *Genesis 22:21-22*

**Marries**

**Rebekah** *Genesis 24*    **Laban** *Genesis 24:29*

**Esau** *Genesis 25:25-26*    **Jacob** m ▬ **Leah** m ▬ **Rachel** c ▬ **Bilhah** c ▬ **Zilpah**
        *Israel*    *Genesis 29, 30*    *Genesis 30, 35*    *Genesis 30*    *Genesis 30*

| Reuben | Simeon | Levi | Judah | Issachar | Zebulun | Dinah | Joseph | Benjamin | Dan | Naphtali | Gad | Asher |
|---|---|---|---|---|---|---|---|---|---|---|---|---|
| 1 | 2 | 3 | 4 | 9 | 10 | *Genesis 46:15* | 11 | 12 | 5 | 6 | 7 | 8 |

The family of Jacob in Paddan-aram *Genesis 35:23-26*
Sons are shown numbered in order of birth

▬ **m** = married
▬ **c** = concubine
       or maidservant

**Ephraim** *Genesis 46:20*    **Manasseh**

Shrine built over the traditional site in Hebron of the Cave of Machpelah, burial place of the Patriarchs.

# What happened to the Israelites during the Exodus?

**1.** The Israelites are told to leave Egypt by the Pharaoh, probably Rameses II. The years of slavery are over. *Exodus 12:29-36*

**2.** They travel to the region of the Bitter Lakes. *Exodus 12:37-39; 13:17–14:4*

**3.** Rameses changes his mind and pursues his escaped slaves. He traps the Israelites at the sea. *Exodus 14:5-12*

**4.** God tells Moses to hold out his stick over the sea. The waters are driven back and the people cross on dry land. The Egyptians are drowned as the water returns. *Exodus 14:13-31*

**5.** After three days they arrive at Marah – but the water is too bitter to drink. *Exodus 15:22-26*

**6.** God first provides manna and quails to eat. *Exodus 16*

**7.** God provides water from a rock. The Amalekites attack and are defeated. Moses' father-in-law advises Moses. *Exodus 17–18*

**8.** Israel receives the Law from God at Mount Sinai. *Exodus 19–32*

**9.** Miriam becomes leprous for her jealousy and rebellion against Moses. *Numbers 12:1-16*

**10.** Eleven days after leaving Mount Sinai, Moses sends twelve spies into Canaan. *Numbers 13:1-24*

**11.** The spies return. Ten bring bad reports, leading the people to rebellion. They want a new leader to take them back to Egypt. *Numbers 13:5–14:10*

**12.** As punishment, God sends them to wander in the desert forty years before entering Canaan. *Numbers 14:11-38*

**Cliffs in the Negev.**

# The judges, the kings and the prophets

## The Twelve Tribes of Israel

| | |
|---|---|
| Reuben | Gad |
| Judah | Joseph |
| Dan | Levi |
| Naphtali | Issachar |
| Simeon | Asher |
| Zebulun | Benjamin |

Worship site at Dan.

## Who were the judges of Israel and their adversaries?

| Judge / *Oppressor* | Actions | Years the judge led Israel / *Years of oppression* | Reference in book of Judges |
|---|---|---|---|
| *Cushan, king of Aram* | | *8* | *3:8* |
| Othniel | Freed Israel from Mesopotamian oppressors | 40 | *3:7-11* |
| *Eglon, king of Moab* | | *18* | *3:14* |
| Ehud | Freed Israel from Moabite oppressors | 80 | *3:12-30* |
| Shamgar | Freed Israel from Philistine oppressors | 10 | *3:31* |
| *Jabin, king of Canaan* | | *20* | *4:3* |
| Deborah | Deborah the only woman judge<br>With Barak, freed Israel from Canaanite oppressors | 40 | *4:4–5:31* |
| *Midianites* | | *7* | *6:1* |
| Gideon | Sought a sign from God<br>Freed Israel from Midianite oppressors | 40 | *6:11–8:35* |
| *Abimelech* | *Terrorized the people as self-proclaimed king of Israel* | *3* | *9* |
| Tola | | 23 | *10:1-2* |
| Jair | | 22 | *10:3-5* |
| *Ammonites* | | *18* | *10:7-9* |
| Jephthah | Freed Israel from Ammonite oppressors | 6 | *10:6–12:7* |
| Ibzan | | 7 | *12:8-10* |
| Elon | | 10 | *12:11-12* |
| Abdon | | 8 | *12:13-15* |
| *Philistines* | | *40* | *13:1* |
| Samson | Famous for his remarkable strength | 20 | *13-16* |
| Eli | Priest and judge | 40 | *1 Samuel 1:1–4:18* |
| Samuel | Prophet and judge | 21 | *1 Samuel 1:11–13:15* |
| Joel/Abijah | | | *1 Samuel 8:1-2* |

# Who were the kings and prophets of Judah and Israel?

| Judah King | Judah Prophet | Date BC | Israel King | Israel Prophet | Assyria |
|---|---|---|---|---|---|
| Rehoboam | Shemaiah | 931 | Jeroboam I | Ahijah | |
| *Egypt invades Jerusalem* | | | | | |
| Abijah | Iddo | 913 | *War with Judah* | | |
| Asa | Azariah | 911 | | | |
| | Hanani | 910 | Nadab | | |
| | | 909 | Baasha | Jehu | |
| *Allies with Syria against Baasha* | | 886 | Elah | | |
| | | 885 | Zimri | | |
| | | 885 | Tibni* | | |
| | | 885 | Omri | | 883–859 Ashurnasirpal II |
| | | | *Samaria becomes capital* | | |
| | | 874 | Ahab | Elijah, Micaiah | |
| Jehoshaphat | Jehu | 870 | *Allies with Judah against Syria* | | |
| | Jahaziel | 853 | Ahaziah | Elisha | 858–824 Shalmaneser III |
| | Eliezer | 852 | Jehoram  Joram | | |
| Jehoram  Joram | | 848 | | | |
| Ahaziah | | 841 | Jehu | | |
| Athaliah | | 841 | | | |
| Jehoash  Joash | Joel | 835 | | | |
| | Zechariah | 814 | Jehoahaz | | |
| | | 798 | Jehoash  Joash | | |
| Amaziah | | 796 | *Fights Amaziah* | | |
| | | 782 | Jeroboam II | Jonah | 782–773 Shalmaneser IV |
| Uzziah  Azariah | | 767 | | Amos | |
| | Isaiah | 753 | Zechariah | Hosea | |
| Jotham regent | | 752 | Shallum | | |
| | | 752 | Menahem | | 744–727 Tiglath-Pileser III |
| | | 742 | Pekahiah | | |
| | | | *Pays tribute to Assyria* | | |
| Jotham | | 740 | Pekah | Oded | |
| | | | *Fights Assyria* | | |
| | | | *Many deported* | | |
| Ahaz | Micah | 732 | Hoshea | | |
| *Tribute to Assyria* | | | *Tribute to Assyria* | | 726–722 Shalmaneser V |
| | | 724 | *Fall of Samaria* | | 721–705 Sargon II |
| Hezekiah | | 715 | | | 704–681 Sennacherib |
| *Sennacherib invades* | | 701 | | | |
| Manasseh | | 687 | | | 680–669 Esarhaddon |
| Amon | | 642 | | | |
| Josiah | Nahum | 640 | | | |
| *Religious reform* | Zephaniah | | | | |
| | Habakkuk | 612 | | | *Nineveh falls* |
| Jehoahaz | Jeremiah | 609 | | | |
| Jehoiakim | Uriah | 609 | | | |
| | | 605 | | | *Egypt loses battle of Carchemish* |
| *Tribute to Egypt* | | | | | |
| Jehoiachin | | 598 | | | |
| *Many deported to Babylon* | | | | | |
| Zedekiah | | 597 | | | |
| *Fall of Jerusalem* | | 587 | | | |

*See 1 Kings 16:21–22*

# The Jewish year

## What Jewish festivals were celebrated in Bible times?

**Passover** (Pesach) and
**Unleavened Bread**
Commemorated Israel's deliverance from Egypt
*Exodus 12:11-30; Leviticus 23:4-8; Numbers 28:16-25; Matthew 26:17*
Each family celebrated the deliverance of the Hebrews from slavery in Egypt, and symbolically re-enacted the first Passover as they ate their own special meal. The celebration continued for seven days as they commemorated the Exodus and wilderness wanderings by eating unleavened bread, recalling the haste with which they left Egypt, when they did not have time to let the bread rise.

**Firstfruits**
*Leviticus 23:9-14; Numbers 28:26-31*
A barley harvest feast at the end of the seven-day Passover festival

**Second Passover**
*Numbers 9:9-13; 2 Chronicles 30:2-3*
For those unable to keep the first Passover

**Pentecost**
(Shavuot, Weeks, Firstfruits, Harvest)
A celebration of harvest
*Leviticus 23:9-22; Deuteronomy 16:9-12; Acts 2:1*
At Pentecost, seven weeks after Passover, the Jews celebrated the gathering in of the wheat harvest. The priests offered symbolically two loaves made from new flour. This feast also celebrated the giving of the Law to Moses at Mount Sinai.

**Trumpets** (Rosh Hashanah, New Year, Judgment and Memorial)
A time of reckoning with God
*Leviticus 23:23-25; Numbers 29:1-6*
This two-day celebration marked by the blowing of trumpets to greet the civil new year, was also the beginning of the most solemn month in the year. The Israelites prepared themselves for Yom Kippur, which comes ten days later, by praising God, whose standard they had failed to meet, and recounting his greatness, love and mercy.

**Day of Atonement**
(Yom ha-Kippurim, Yom Kippur)
The most holy day in the Jewish year
*Leviticus 16; 23:26-32; Numbers 29:7-11*
On Yom Kippur Israel confessed the nation's sins, and asked forgiveness and cleansing. A scapegoat was sent into the desert, carrying symbolically the people's sin. The high priest entered the Most Holy Place of the Temple on this day alone. Recognizing this day as the holiest of feast days, Jews neither ate nor drank for twenty-four hours.

**Tabernacles**
(Succoth, Booths, Ingathering)
Commemorated Israel's wanderings in the wilderness
*Leviticus 23:33-44; Numbers 29:12-40; John 7:2*
A joyful harvest festival. During the seven-day celebration the people thanked God for protecting them in the wilderness and for the harvest. For seven days they lived in shelters made of branches, to remind them of their time living in tents in the wilderness.

## The Hebrew Calendar

| Month | Name (name before Exile) | Modern equivalent |
|---|---|---|
| 1 | **Nisan** (Abib) | March/April |
| 2 | **Iyyar** (Ziv) | April/May |
| 3 | **Sivan** | May/June |
| 4 | **Tammuz** | June/July |
| 5 | **Abu** (Ab) | July/August |
| 6 | **Elul** | August/September |
| 7 | **Tishri** (Ethanim) | September/October |
| 8 | **Heshvan** (Bul) = Marcheshvan | October/November |
| 9 | **Chislev** | November/December |
| 10 | **Tebeth** | December/January |
| 11 | **Shebat** | January/February |
| 12 | **Adar** | February/March |

*The Jewish year is strictly lunar, with lunar months averaging 29.5 days, giving 354 days in a year. A thirteenth month, Second Adar, was added about every three years to align the calendar with the solar year.*

**A Jewish family celebrate Passover in modern Israel.**

*1 Maccabees 4:41-49;*
*John 10:22*
On Hanukkah the Jews celebrated the expulsion of the Syrians by Judas Maccabeus in 164 BC, and the cleansing and rededication of the Jerusalem Temple, which the Syrians had desecrated. Lighting a new candle each day for eight days, the Jews commemorated the miracle of the Temple's holy candelabrum: for the rededication they had only one day's worth of consecrated oil but it burnt for eight full days, the time required to consecrate more oil.

## The Sabbath
A rest day commanded by God (Exodus 20:8-11), following his own example (Genesis 2:3) and to be a mark of God's people (Exodus 31:13-7). Every seventh day was set aside as the Sabbath. By New Testament times, rules for Sabbath keeping had become very complicated (Isaiah 56; 58:13-14, Matthew 12:1-14).

## Dedication
(Hanukkah, Lights, Maccabees) Commemorated the rededication of the Temple in 164 BC

## Purim (Lots)
Celebrated the failure of Haman's plot to destroy the Jews
*Esther 9:21, 27-28*
A time of feasting and joy when the people celebrated the deliverance of the Jews from death through the bravery of the Jewish Queen Esther of Persia.

| Weather | Harvests/Agriculture | Festivals/Holy Days |
|---|---|---|
| Rain ('latter rain') | Flax harvest | •14th Passover<br>•15th-21st Unleavened Bread<br>•16th Firstfruits |
| Dry | Barley harvest | •14th Second Passover |
| Warm and dry | Wheat harvest | •6th Pentecost<br>(= Harvest, Firstfruits, Shavuot, Weeks) |
| Hot and dry | | |
| Very hot and dry | | |
| Very hot and dry | Date harvest<br>Grape harvest<br>Summer fig harvest | |
| Rain begins | Olive harvest<br>Grape harvest | • 1st Trumpets (= Rosh Hashanah)<br>•10th Day of Atonement (= Yom Kippur)<br>•15th-21st Tabernacles<br>(= Ingathering, Succoth, Booths)<br>•22nd Simhath Torah<br>(= Solemn Assembly) |
| Rainy ('former rain')<br>Ploughing | Olive harvest | |
| Cool and rainy | Winter fig harvest<br>Sowing | •25th-2nd Tebeth Dedication<br>(= Hanukkah, Lights) |
| Cold, hail and snow | Sowing | |
| Warmer and rain | Almond blossoms,<br>Sowing | |
| Thunder and hail | Citrus fruit harvest<br>Sowing | •14th-15th Purim (= Lots) |

# Animal, Vegetable, and Mineral . . .

## Why are some mountains of the Bible important?

| Mount | Height (in feet/meters above sea level) | Bible reference | Biblical significance |
|---|---|---|---|
| Ararat | 16,946/5,165 | *Genesis 8:4* | Noah's ark came to rest |
| Sinai (also called Horeb) | 7,500/2,286 | *Exodus 3,19* *1 Kings 19* | God revealed his name and his Law to Moses. Elijah fled there from Jezebel. |
| Ebal | 3,100/945 | *Deuteronomy 11:29* | Moses reminded Israel of the Law's blessings and curses |
| Gerizim | 2,900/884 | | |
| Nebo | 2,700/823 | *Deuteronomy 32:49* | Moses died here |
| Halak | 1,640/500 | *Joshua 11:17* | Southern boundary of Joshua's conquest |
| Hermon | 9,100/2,774 | *Joshua 11:17* *Matthew 17:1* | Northern boundary of Joshua's conquest ?Jesus transfigured here |
| Tabor | 1,900/580 | *Judges 4:6* *Matthew 17:1* | Deborah's forces fought Sisera ?Jesus was transfigured here |
| Gilboa | 1,700/518 | *1 Samuel 31:1* | Saul killed in battle |
| Carmel | 1,750/535 | *1 Kings 18:20* | Elijah defeated prophets of Baal |
| Moriah | | *2 Chronicles 3:1* | Early name for Mount Zion |
| Zion | | *Psalm 48:1, 2* | Site of the temple |
| Temptation | | *Luke 4:5* | Jesus was tempted by Satan |
| Beatitudes | | *Matthew 5–7* | Jesus' Sermon on the Mount |
| Olives | 2,600/811 | *Zechariah 14:4* *Matthew 26:30* | Site of Bethany, Gethsemane, Jesus' ascension, and his predicted return |

**The foothills of Mount Hermon, northern Palestine.**

## Some animals in the Bible

**Antelope** *Deuteronomy 14:5*
**Ape** *2 Chronicles 9:21*
**Baboon** *2 Chronicles 9:21*
**Bat** *Leviticus 11:19*
**Bear** *1 Samuel 17:34-36*
**Boar** *Psalm 80:13*
**Camel** *Job 1:3*
**Cattle** *Genesis 12:16*
**Coney,** or rock badger *Deuteronomy 14:7*
**Deer** *Deuteronomy 12:15*
**Dog** *1 Samuel 17:43*
**Donkey** *Genesis 12:16*
**Fox** *Song of Solomon 2:15*
**Gazelle** *Deuteronomy 12:15*
**Goat** *Genesis 27:9*
**Horse** *Genesis 47:17*
**Hyena** *Isaiah 34:14*
**Ibex** *Deuteronomy 14:5*
**Jackal** *Isaiah 34:13*
**Leopard** *Jeremiah 13:23*
**Lion** *Judges 14:5-6*
**Mule** *1 Kings 1:33*
**Ox** *Deuteronomy 14:4*
**Pig** *Leviticus 11:7*
**Rabbit** *Leviticus 11:6*
**Rat** *Leviticus 11:29*
**Roe deer** *Deuteronomy 14:5*
**Sheep** *1 Samuel 16:11*
**Weasel** *Leviticus 11 :29*
**Wild goat** *Deuteronomy 14:5*
**Wolf** *Matthew 7:15*

Camels from an Assyrian relief.

## Musical instruments of the Bible

| Instrument | Hebrew | Bible references |
|---|---|---|
| **Wind** | | |
| Ram's horn | *shophar, yobel* | *Exodus 19:13; Psalm 81:3; Joshua 6:4* |
| Trumpet | *hasoserah* | *Numbers 10:2-10; Psalm 150:3* |
| Flute | *'ugab* | *Job 21:12; 30:31; Luke 7:32* |
| Double pipe | *halil* | *1 Kings 1:40; Isaiah 5:12* |
| **String** | | |
| Lyre | *nebel* | *2 Samuel 6:5; Psalm 33:2* |
| Harp | *kinnor* | *Genesis 31:27; Psalm 43:4* |
| **Percussion** | | |
| Tambourine | *toph* | *Exodus 15:20; 1 Samuel 18:6; Psalm 149:3* |
| Cymbals | *selselim, mesiltayim* | *1 Chronicles 13:8; Psalm 150:5; Nehemiah 12:27;* |

## Some birds in the Bible

**Black kite** *Leviticus 11:14*
**Cormorant** *Leviticus 11:17*
**Desert owl** *Leviticus 11:18*
**Dove** *Genesis 8:8*
**Eagle** *Leviticus 11:13*
**Falcon** *Deuteronomy 14:13*
**Great owl** *Leviticus 11:17*
**Gull** *Leviticus 11:16*
**Hawk** *Leviticus 11:16*
**Hen** *Matthew 23:37*
**Heron** *Leviticus 11:19*
**Horned owl** *Leviticus 11:16*
**Osprey** *Leviticus 11:18*
**Owl** *Leviticus 11:17*
**Partridge** *Jeremiah 17:11*
**Pigeon** *Luke 2:24*
**Quail** *Exodus 16:13*
**Raven** *Genesis 8:7*
**Red kite** *Leviticus 11:14*
**Rooster** *Matthew 26:34*
**Screech owl** *Isaiah 34:11*
**Sparrow** *Psalm 84:3*
**Stork** *Leviticus 11:19*
**Swallow** *Psalm 84:3*
**Swift** *Isaiah 38:14*
**Thrush** *Isaiah 38:14*
**Vulture** *Leviticus 11:13*
**White owl** *Leviticus 11:18*

*The exact identity of many of the items listed on this page is uncertain.*

*Even the sparrow finds a home and the swallow a nest for herself ...*
*Psalm*

# The Exile and After ...

## The three Jewish Returns from Exile

|  | First Return<br>Ezra 1–6 | Second Return<br>Ezra 7–10 | Third Return<br>Nehemiah 1–2 |
|---|---|---|---|
| **Scripture** | Ezra 1–6 | Ezra 7–10 | Nehemiah 1–2 |
| **Date** | 538 BC | 458 BC | 445 BC |
| **King of Persia** | Cyrus the Great 550–529 | Artaxerxes I 465–425 | Artaxerxes I |
| **Leader of return** | Zerubbabel | Ezra | Nehemiah |
| **Leader's role** | Governor | Priest | Governor |
| **Number of returnees** | 49,897 | 1,774 | Armed escort |
| **Other leaders at the time** | Joshua the priest<br>Haggai, Zechariah | Nehemiah, Malachi | Ezra, Malachi |
| **Result** | Temple foundations laid<br>Walls rebuilt<br>Work stops | Law taught | Jerusalem's people<br>separated from non-Jews |

## Rulers of the Persian Empire

**Cyrus II "the Great" 550–529**
The conqueror of Babylon, Cyrus II reversed previous policy and returned exiled peoples to their homelands. By his decree, the Jews returned to Judea.
*2 Chronicles 36:22, 23; Ezra 1–6; Isaiah 44:28; 45:1; Daniel 10:1*

**Cambyses II 529–522**

**Darius I 522–486**
Darius I, a strong ruler, confirmed the decree of Cyrus II and ordered the Jerusalem temple to be completed at Persian expense.
*Ezra 5:3–6:15; Nehemiah 12:22; Haggai 1:1; Zechariah 1:1*

**Xerxes I 486–465**
Xerxes I, probably Ahasuerus in the book of Esther, failed in two attempts to invade Greece.
*Esther*

**Artaxerxes I 465–425** Nehemiah was cupbearer to Artaxerxes I, who granted his request and made him governor of Judea. During his rule the walls of Jerusalem were rebuilt.
*Ezra 7:1, 21–26; Nehemiah 2:1–8*

**Xerxes II 425–424**

**Darius II 423–404**

**Artaxerxes II 404–359**

**Artaxerxes II 359–338**

**Arses 338–336**

**Darius II 336–330**

*All dates are approximate and BC*

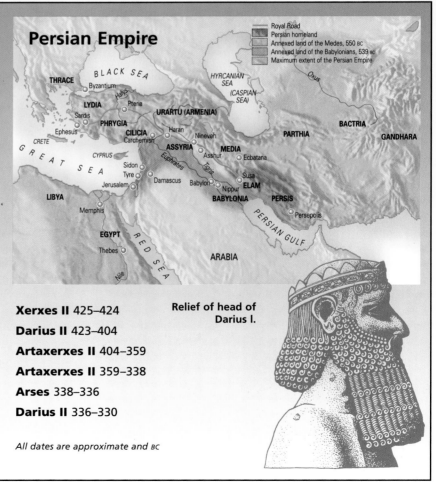

### Persian Empire

Royal Road
Persian homeland
Annexed land of the Medes, 550 BC
Annexed land of the Babylonians, 539 BC
Maximum extent of the Persian Empire

THRACE
BLACK SEA
Byzantium
HYRCANIAN SEA (CASPIAN SEA)
Oxus
LYDIA
Pteria
Sardis
Halys
URARTU (ARMENIA)
Ephesus
PHRYGIA
Haran
Nineveh
PARTHIA
BACTRIA
CRETE
CILICIA
Carchemish
ASSYRIA
Asshur
MEDIA
Ecbatana
GANDHARA
CYPRUS
Sidon
Euphrates
Tigris
Susa
GREAT SEA
Tyre
Damascus
Babylon
ELAM
Jerusalem
Nippur
LIBYA
BABYLONIA
PERSIS
Memphis
PERSIAN GULF
Persepolis
EGYPT
RED SEA
Thebes
ARABIA
Nile

**Relief of head of Darius I.**

# What does the Old Testament Apocrypha consist of?

The Apocrypha or Deuterocanonical literature is a collection of books and additions to Old Testament books written between 300 BC and AD 100. Many of these books are found in the Greek version of the Jewish Bible (the Septuagint). From there they passed into the Christian Old Testament of the Catholic and Orthodox traditions. However, in the first century A.D. they were rejected by the Jews as Scripture and so did not find a place in the Hebrew Bible, which is the basis of the Old Testament, according to the Protestant tradition. The books of the Apocrypha are interesting, and valuable as historical documents, and range from narrative history to pious fiction.

### 1 Esdras
An historical account, paralleling parts of Chronicles, Ezra and Nehemiah, of the return of the Jews from Babylonian captivity.

### 2 Esdras (4 Ezra)
Apocalyptic work dealing with problem of divine justice in the light of destruction of the temple in A.D.70.

### Tobit
A didactic fiction about the trials of Tobit, a righteous Jew, who lived in eighth century BC Nineveh.

### Judith
The fictional exploits of a Jewish heroine, Judith, who assassinated the Assyrian general Holofernes.

### Additions to Esther (also known as The Rest of Esther)
Five additions which give a more religious emphasis to the book of Esther.

### The Wisdom of Solomon
A first century BC exhortation to wisdom.

### Ecclesiasticus also known as the Wisdom of Sirach/Ben Sira
A collection of the writings of Jesus (Jeshua) ben-Sira (about 180 BC) giving his advice for a successful life – combining personal piety with practical wisdom.

### Baruch (1 Baruch)
This book was allegedly written by Baruch, a friend of Jeremiah, and was meant as an encouragement to Jews in the Babylonian exile of 597 BC.

### The Letter of Jeremiah
An attack on idolatry in the form of a letter from Jeremiah, often added to the book of Baruch.

### The Song of the Three Holy Children
A hymn of praise sung by Shadrach, Meshach and Abednego in the fiery furnace described in Daniel.

### The Story of Susanna
The story of a virtuous woman who was falsely accused of adultery and defended by Daniel.

### Bel and the Dragon
A folkloric story written to ridicule idolatry.

### The Prayer of Manasseh
The prayer of the idolatrous king Manasseh, begging for forgiveness, as referred to in 2 Chronicles 33:11-19.

### 1 Maccabees
The struggle of Jews against Hellenistic rulers (175-134 BC), particularly the battle with Antiochus Epiphanes.

### 2 Maccabees
A narrative of the Maccabean revolt.

### 3 Maccabees
An account of Jewish life under Ptolemy IV (221-204 BC).

### 4 Maccabees
A tract about the rule of reason over passion, set against the background of cruel martyrdom.

### Psalm 151

## What is the Septuagint?

Alexandria, the capital of Egypt under the Ptolemies, had a large community of Jews who could no longer understand Hebrew well. They wanted a Greek translation of their Scriptures, and tradition has it that 72 scholars were sent from Jerusalem to complete the work. The translation became known as the Septuagint (= 70), sometimes written as LXX (70 in Roman numerals). To begin with, only the first five books of the Old Testament were included, but other books were added later.

ΚΑΙΔΟΘΗΤΩϹΜΗΓ
ΜΑΚΑΙΗΛΟΙΠΗΕ
ΙΙΙΜΕΛΙΑΚΑΙΤΥΝΙΙ
ΗΑΝΑΡΕϹΗ ΤΩΒΑϹΙ
ΛΕΙΚΑϹΙΛΕΥϹΕΙΑΝ
ΤΙΑϹΤΙΝΚΑΙΗΡΕϹΕ
ΤΩΒΑϹΙΛΕΙΤΟΓΙΡΑ
ΓΜΑΚΑΙΕΓΟΙΗϹΕ

# Varieties of religion in Bible times

## False gods of Bible times

| Name | Where worshipped | Description | Scripture |
|---|---|---|---|
| Artemis (Diana) | Asia | many-breasted fertility goddess | *Acts 19:28* |
| Asherah  symbol – a pole | Canaan | goddess of the sea  wife of El | *Judges 3:7*  *1 Kings 18:19*  *2 Kings 21:3*  *2 Chronicles 15:16; 24:18* |
| Ashtoreth (Astarte Queen of Heaven) | Canaan  Sidon | mother-goddess;  fertility goddess | *Judges 2:13; 10:6*  *1 Samuel 12:10*  *1 Kings 11:5, 33*  *Jeremiah 7:18; 44:17-25* |
| Baal | Canaan | young storm god  chief god of Canaan until the Exile; the name Baal is often linked with place names, such as Gad, Peor, etc. | *Judges 2:13;*  *1 Kings 16:31-32;18:18-29* |
| Baal-Zebub | Philistia | god of Ekron | *2 Kings 1:2* |
| Castor, Pollux | Greece | twin sons of Zeus | *Acts 28:11* |
| Chemosh | Moab  ?Ammon | national god of war | *Numbers 21:29*  *Judges 11:24*  *1 Kings 11:7, 33*  *Jeremiah 48:7* |
| Dagon | Philistia | national god of rain/agriculture | *Judges 16:23*  *1 Samuel 5:2-7* |
| Hermes (Mercury) | Greece | messenger god, god of cunning, theft | *Acts 14:12* |
| Marduk (Bel) | Babylon | young storm/war god  chief god | *Isaiah 46:1*  *Jeremiah 50:2; 51:44* |
| Molech (Malcam) (Milcom) (Moloch) (?Rephan) | Ammon  Israel | national god  worshipped with child sacrifice | *Zephaniah 1:5*  *Jeremiah 49:1, 3*  *Kings 11:5, 7, 33*  *Acts 7:43*  *Acts 7:43* |
| Nebo (Nabu) | Babylon | son of Marduk  god of wisdom, literature, arts | *Isaiah 46:1* |
| Nergal | Babylon | god of hunting/the underworld | *2 Kings 17:30* |
| Rimmon (Hadad) | Damascus | god of thunder, lightning, rain | *2 Kings 5:18* |
| Tammuz | Babylon | fertility god | *Ezekiel 8:14* |
| Zeus | Greece | chief of Greek gods | *Acts 14:12* |

( ) = alternative name

# Some Jewish groups mentioned in the New Testament

## RELIGIOUS

### Pharisees
This group probably emerged, like the Essenes, from supporters of the Maccobeans in the revolt against Antiochus. They studied the law of the Pentateuch (the written Law) and also conserved and develped additional teachings based on the Pentateuch (oral law), intended to make the laws of the Bible applicable to the ever-changeing circumstances of the people of Israel. Like all other groups of the time, they believed themselves to be the only true upholders of God's covenant with Israel. The name 'Pharisees' might originally have meant 'seperated ones'. It is clear that the Pharisees were influential in New Testament times, and the Gospels portray the relationship between them and Jesus as often bitter.

### Sadducees
A small Jewish sect made up mainly of priests and members of the Sanhedrin council (*Acts 4:1; 5:17*). Their dislike of all change and a desire to keep everything as it was led to frequent quarrels with the Pharisees. The name 'Sadducee' probably means 'heir of Zadok'. (priest of David and Solomon). They believed that the Mosaic Law was the supreme authority, and that no oral law or tradition was equal to Scripture. In contrast to the Pharisees, they did not believe in a resurrection, angels or spirits (*Mark 12:18; Acts 23:8*). The Sadducees kept on good terms with the Romans when they came to power.

### Essenes
A Jewish sect whose members lived a form of monastic life. Sometimes living in isolated communities such as Qumran (near to where the Dead Sea Scrolls were discovered), their name might mean 'pious ones'. If some of the Dead Sea Scrolls are Essene works, then it appears that the Essenes believed in an imminent final battle between good and evil and devoted themselves to the study and interpretation of scripture and to the worship of God alongside the angels.

## POLITICAL

### Herodians
A sect of Jews who agreed to subject themselves to Roman rule. They believed that Herod and his descendants were the last hope for Israel to maintain their own national government. They helped plot the death of Jesus (*Mark 12:13; Matthew 22:16*).

### Zealots
A strongly nationalistic Jewish sect whose slogan was: 'No Lord but Jehovah.' They combined the religious practices of the Pharisees with hatred for any non-Jewish government (*Matthew 10:4*).

### Galileans
A sect that believed that foreign control of Israel was against Scripture, and therefore refused to acknowledge foreign rulers. Similar politically to the Zealots, the Galileans were eventually absorbed into that sect (*Acts 5:37*).

## SOCIAL

### Scribes
Jewish men who copied, taught and explained the Law. Many Scribes were Pharisees, and, like them, believed in the authority of oral traditions (*Luke 20:46*). As teachers of the Law, they were important in Jewish society, and also served as judges or lawyers.

### Nazirites
Jews who took a vow of separation for a limited time or for life. Easily recognized because they vowed never to cut their hair, Nazirites separated themselves by their lifestyle to be close to God (*Numbers 6:2, 4-6; Judges 13:5; 1 Samuel 1:11; Acts 18:18; 21:23-24*).

### Proselytes
A non-Jew who had been converted to Judaism. By being circumcised, a convert was thought to have joined the family of Abraham and was expected to follow the Law.

### Publicans
Jews who collected taxes for the Roman government. Their willingness to work in the government was seen as disloyal to Israel (*Luke 19:1-9*).

Some of the Levites (Temple assistants) served as Temple guards.

Pharisee.

Sadducee.

High Priest.

# The Political Background of Jesus' Life

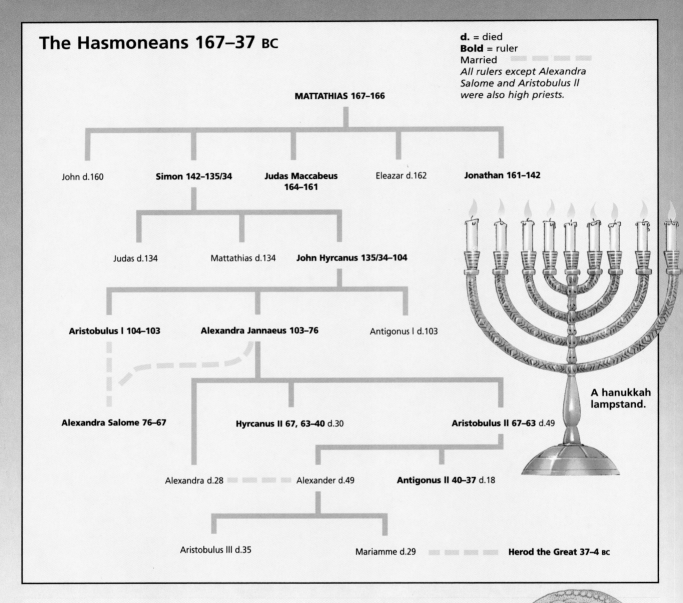

## The Hasmoneans 167–37 BC

d. = died
**Bold** = ruler
Married ▬ ▬ ▬ ▬
*All rulers except Alexandra Salome and Aristobulus II were also high priests.*

**MATTATHIAS 167–166**

John d.160 — **Simon 142–135/34** — **Judas Maccabeus 164–161** — Eleazar d.162 — **Jonathan 161–142**

Judas d.134 — Mattathias d.134 — **John Hyrcanus 135/34–104**

**Aristobulus I 104–103** — **Alexandra Jannaeus 103–76** — Antigonus I d.103

**Alexandra Salome 76–67** — **Hyrcanus II 67, 63–40 d.30** — **Aristobulus II 67–63 d.49**

Alexandra d.28 ▬ ▬ ▬ Alexander d.49 — **Antigonus II 40–37 d.18**

Aristobulus III d.35 — Mariamme d.29 ▬ ▬ ▬ **Herod the Great 37–4 BC**

A hanukkah lampstand.

## Roman Official Posts in New Testament Times

| | |
|---|---|
| **Caesar** | Family name of Julius Caesar taken by Augustus and used as a title for the emperor from that time. *Luke 2:1; 3:1* |
| **Proconsul** | Governor of a province administered by the Roman Senate. *Acts 13:7; 18:12* |
| **Procurator** | Imperial financial agent in a Senate province, or governor of a minor province under an imperial legate. *Matthew 27:11; Acts 23:24; 24:27* |
| **Tribune** | High-ranking military officer in charge of up to 1,000 men. *Acts 21:31* |
| **Centurion** | Officer in charge of 100 men. *Mark 15:39; Acts 10:1* |

# Who were the Roman emperors of Bible times?

| Name | Reign | Christian events | Bible reference |
|---|---|---|---|
| Julius | 49–44 BC | | |
| Augustus | 27 BC–AD 14 | Birth of Jesus | *Luke 2:1* |
| Tiberius | AD 14–37 | Ministry and death of Jesus | *Luke 3:1* |
| Caligula | AD 37–41 | | |
| Claudius | AD 41–54 | Jews expelled from Rome | *Acts 11:28; 18:2* |
| Nero | AD 54–68 | Trial of Paul Persecution at Rome | *Acts 25:10–12; 27:24* |
| Galba | AD 68–69 | | |
| Otho | AD 69 | | |
| Vitellius | AD 69 | | |
| Vespasian | AD 69–79 | Jerusalem destroyed | |
| Titus | AD 79–81 | | |
| Domitian | AD 81–96 | ?Persecution | |
| Nerva | AD 96–98 | | |
| Trajan | AD 98–117 | | |
| Hadrian | AD 117–138 | | |

## Dating

The first Christian calendar, dividing history into BC (before Christ) and AD (*anno domini*, "in the year of our Lord") was worked out by a monk in the sixth century AD. But it has now been discovered that he was about five years out in his calculations, so Jesus was born about 5 BC—not AD 1—towards the end of the reign of Herod the Great.

Traditional site of Jesus' birth, Church of the Nativity, Bethlehem.

# Herod the Great and His Family

**Herod the Great**
37–4 BC
*Matthew 2:1–22; Luke 1:5*

1 Doris

2 Mariamme I

3 Mariamme II

4 Malthace

5 Cleopatra of Jerusalem

5 other wives

**Antipater III**
d.4 BC

**Alexander**
d.7 BC

**Aristobulus**
d.7 BC

**Herod Philip**
*Matthew 14:3*
*Mark 6:17*
*Luke 3:19*

**Archelaus Ethnarch of Judea**
4 BC–AD 6 d.AD 18
*Matthew 2:22*

**Herod Antipas Tetrarch of Galilee**
4 BC–AD 39
*Matthew 14:1–10*
*Mark 6:14–28*
*Luke 3:1,19*

**Philip the Tetrarch of Ituraea**
4 BC–AD 34
*Luke 3:1*

**Herodias**
*Matthew 14:3–11*
*Mark 6:17–28*
*Luke 3:19*

**Herod Agrippa I**
AD 41–44
*Acts 12*

**Herod II King of Chalcis**
AD 41–48

**Salome**
*Matthew 14:6–11*
*Mark 6:22–28*

**Agrippa II King of Chalcis**
AD 50–93
*Acts 25:13–26:32*

**Bernice**
*Acts 25:13–26:32*

**Drusilla**
*Acts 24:24*

**Antonius Felix Procurator of Judea**
AD 52–60

Married — — — —

1. First marriage of Herodias.

2. Second marriage of Herodias

3. Salome, daughter of Herodias and Herod (sometimes referred to as Philip), danced before Herod Antipas for John the Baptist's head. She married her great-uncle Philip the Tetrarch.

d. = died

19

# Four Gospels . . . One Life

## Jesus' Life
### A Simple Harmonization of the Gospels

| | Matthew | Mark | Luke | John |
|---|---|---|---|---|
| **Jesus' birth and childhood  4/5 BC** | | | | |
| Jesus' genealogy | 1:1–17 | | 3:23–38 | |
| Jesus' birth is foretold | 1:18–25 | | 1:26–38 | |
| Jesus is born | 2:1–12 | | 2:1–39 | |
| Jesus' childhood and visit to temple | | | 2:40–52 | |
| | | | | |
| **Jesus prepares for his public ministry AD 29** | | | | |
| Jesus is baptized | 3:13–17 | 1:9–11 | 3:21–22 | |
| Jesus is tempted in the wilderness | 4:1–11 | 1:12–13 | 4:1–13 | |
| | | | | |
| **Jesus' ministry begins** | | | | |
| John points to Jesus | | | | 1:19–34 |
| John's disciples attracted | | | | 1:35–51 |
| The first miracle: water into wine | | | | 2:1–11 |
| "You must be born again" | | | | 3:1–21 |
| | | | | |
| **Jesus in Galilee** | | | | |
| Jesus arrives in Galilee | 4:12–17 | 1:14 | 4:14 | 4:43–45 |
| Jesus calls the first of the Twelve | 4:18–22 | 1:16–20 | 5:1–11 | |
| Many miracles | 8:1–17 | 1:40–2:12 | 5:12–26 | |
| The Sermon on the Mount | 5:1–7:29 | | 6:20–49 | |
| Jesus speaks in parables | 13:1–53 | 4:1–34 | 8:4–18 | |
| A series of miracles | 8:23–9:8, 18–26 | 4:35–5:43 | 8:22–56 | |
| Jesus affirmed as Christ and Son of God | 16:13–26 | 8:27–9:1 | 9:18–27 | |
| Jesus is transfigured | 16:27–17:13 | 9:2–13 | 9:28–36 | |
| Jesus predicts his death and resurrection | 17:22–23 | 9:31–32 | 9:43–45 | |
| Jesus' last Galilean ministry | 17:24–18:35 | 9:33–50 | 9:46–50 | 7:1–9 |
| | | | | |
| **Jesus in Judea and Perea** | | | | |
| Jesus' journey to Jerusalem | 19:1–2 | 10:1 | 9:51–62 | 7:10 |
| Jesus claims deity | | | | 8:12–59 |
| Jesus the Good Shepherd | | | | 10:1–21 |
| Parable of the good Samaritan | | | 10:25–37 | |
| Jesus in Mary and Martha's home | | | 10:38–42 | |
| Jesus teaches a prayer | | | 11:1–13 | |
| Jesus raises Lazarus | | | | 11:1–44 |
| | | | | |
| **Jesus travels towards Jerusalem** | | | | |
| The rich young ruler | 19:16–30 | 10:17–31 | 18:18–30 | |
| Jesus predicts his death | 20:17–19 | 10:32–34 | 18:31–34 | |
| Jesus arrives at Bethany | | | | 11:55–12:11 |

# Who wrote the New Testament?

| Name | Nationality | Occupation | Writings | How he died |
|------|-------------|------------|----------|-------------|
| **Matthew** | Jewish | Tax-collector | Gospel of Matthew | By tradition martyred in Ethiopia |
| **Mark** | Jewish | | Gospel of Mark | By tradition martyred |
| **Luke** | Greek | Physician | Gospel of Luke Acts | By tradition martyred in Greece |
| **John** | Jewish | Fisherman | Gospel of John 1, 2, & 3 John Revelation | Banished to Patmos; natural death |
| **Paul** | Jewish | Pharisee/ Tentmaker | Romans 1 & 2 Corinthians Galatians Ephesians Philippians Colossians 1 & 2 Thessalonians 1 & 2 Timothy, Titus Philemon | By tradition martyred in Rome by Nero |
| **James** | Jewish | | James | By tradition martyred |
| **Peter** | Jewish | Fisherman | 1 & 2 Peter | By tradition crucified upside-down in Rome by Nero |
| **Jude** | Jewish | | Jude | By tradition martyred |

# Who were Jesus' disciples?

**Simon Peter** (Cephas)
*Matthew 14:25–33;
16:13–18; Mark 14:27–39;
Luke 22:54–62; John
20:1–6; 21; Acts 3:1–26;
10:1–48*

**Andrew,** brother of
Simon Peter
*Mark 1:16–18; 3:14–19;
John 1:40–44; Acts 1:13*

**James,** son of Zebedee
*Matthew 10:2; Mark
10:35–41; Acts 12:2*

**John,** brother of James
*Mark 1:19–20; 9:2;
14:33–34; Acts 3:1–11*

**Philip,** of Bethsaida
*Matthew 10:2–3; John
1:43–48; 12:21–22; 14:8–9*

**Bartholomew** (also
called Nathanael)
*Matthew 10:2–3; Luke
6:13–15; John 1:43–51*

**Thomas,** or Didymus,
the "twin"
*John 11:16; 14:5–7;
20:24–29; 21:2*

**Matthew** (also called
Levi)
*Matthew 9:9–10; 10:3*

**James,** son of Alphaeus,
possibly Jesus' cousin
*Matthew 10:3*

**Judas** (Lebbaeus), also
known as Thaddaeus
*Matthew 10:3; Mark 3:18*

**Simon the Zealot** (a
member of the Jewish
resistance movement)
*Matthew 10:4*

**Judas Iscariot** (perhaps
a member of the
extremist group of
"dagger-men" pledged
to kill Romans)
*Matthew 26:47–50; John
13:26–30*

# Who are the Marys of the New Testament?

**Mary, mother of Jesus**
The Jewish woman from
Nazareth whom God chose to
give birth to his son. Married to
Joseph, she was a descendant of
David. Mary stood at the foot of
the cross when Jesus was killed.
*Matthew 1:18–25; Luke 1:26–45;
John 19:25–27; Acts 1:14*

**Mary of Bethany**
With her sister Martha and
brother Lazarus, a close friend of
Jesus, whose feet she anointed
with perfume.
*Luke 10:38–42; John 11:1–45;
12:1–3; compare Matthew 26:7;
Mark 14:3*

**Mary, mother of James
and Joseph** (Joses)
A Galilean woman who, after
being healed, followed Jesus
and supported his ministry
financially.
*Matthew 27:56; 28:1;
Mark 15:40, 41, 47*

**Mary Magdalene**
Another Galilean woman whom
Jesus healed, and who helped to
support Jesus' ministry.
*Matthew 27:56, 61; 28:1; Mark
15:40, 47; 16:1, 9; Luke 8:2;
John 20:1, 2, 11–18*

**Mary, mother of John Mark**
A relative of Barnabas; her home
was a gathering place for the
Jerusalem church.
*Acts 12:12, 13; Colossians 4:10*

**Mary of Rome**
A woman commended by Paul.
*Romans 16:6*

# Jesus' Words and Deeds

## Miracles of Jesus

### Healing of Individuals

| Healing of Individuals | Matthew | Mark | Luke | John |
|---|---|---|---|---|
| Son of government official | | | | 4:46–54 |
| Sick man at a pool | | | | 5:1–15 |
| Man in synagogue | | 1:21–28 | 4:31–37 | |
| Man with skin-disease | 8:1–4 | 1:40–45 | 5:12–14 | |
| Roman officer's servant | 8:5–13 | | 7:1–10 | |
| Dead son of a widow | | | 7:11–15 | |
| Peter's mother-in-law | 8:14–15 | 1:29–31 | 4:38–39 | |
| An uncontrollable man | 8:28–34 | 5:1–20 | 8:26–39 | |
| Paralyzed man | 9:1–7 | 2:1–12 | 5:17–26 | |
| Woman with severe bleeding | 9:20–22 | 5:25–34 | 8:43–48 | |
| Dead girl | 9:18–26 | 5:21–43 | 8:40–56 | |
| Dumb man | 9:32–34 | | | |
| Man with a paralyzed hand | 12:9–14 | 3:1–6 | 6:6–11 | |
| Blind and dumb man | 12:22 | | 11:14 | |
| Canaanite woman's daughter | 15:21–28 | 7:24–30 | | |
| Deaf and dumb man | | 7:31–37 | | |
| Blind man at Bethsaida | | 8:22–26 | | |
| Boy with epilepsy | 17:14–18 | 9:14–29 | 9:37–43 | |
| Blind Bartimaeus | 20:29–34 | 10:46–52 | 18:35–43 | |
| Woman with a bad back | | | 13:10–17 | |
| Sick man | | | 14:1–6 | |
| Man born blind | | | | 9:1–41 |
| Dead friend named Lazarus | | | | 11:1–44 |
| Slave's ear | | | 22:47–51 | |

### Healing of Groups

| Healing of Groups | Matthew | Mark | Luke | John |
|---|---|---|---|---|
| Crowd in Capernaum | 8:16–17 | 1:32–34 | 4:40–41 | |
| Two blind men | 9:27–31 | | | |
| Crowd by Lake Galilee | | 3:7–12 | | |
| Crowd on the hillside by Lake Galilee | 15:29–31 | | | |
| Ten men | | | 17:11–19 | |

### Control over Laws of Nature

| Control over Laws of Nature | Matthew | Mark | Luke | John |
|---|---|---|---|---|
| Water changed into wine | | | | 2:1–11 |
| Catch of fish | | | 5:1–11 | |
| Jesus calms a storm | 8:23–27 | 4:35–41 | 8:22–25 | |
| Crowds: over 5,000 people fed | 14:13–21 | 6:32–44 | 9:10–17 | 6:1–13 |
| Jesus walks on the water | 14:22–33 | 6:45–52 | | 6:16–21 |
| Crowds: over 4,000 people fed | 15:32–38 | 8:1–10 | | |
| A fish and the payment of taxes | 17:24–27 | | | |
| Fig tree withers away | 21:18–22 | 11:12–14, 20–24 | | |
| Another catch of fish | | | | 21:1–11 |
| Christ conquers death | 28:1–10 | 16:1–11 | 24:1–12 | 20:1–18 |

## Where do we find miracles in the Bible?

Most of the miracles in the Bible are clustered around a few people and events:

• **Moses** and the beginnings of the people of Israel

• **Elijah** and **Elisha** and the beginnings of the line of prophets who recalled their people to their covenant (agreement) with God

• **Jesus** and the beginning of the new Israel

• The **apostles** and the founding of the Christian church

## Ten People Raised from the Dead

**Zarephath widow's son**
*1 Kings 17:17–24*

**Shunammite woman's son** *2 Kings 4:32–37*

**Man whose body touched Elisha's bones**
*2 Kings 13:20–21*

**People at Jesus' death**
*Matthew 27:50–53*

**Jesus**
*Matthew 28:5–8; Mark 16:6; Luke 24:5–7*

**Son of the widow of Nain**
*Luke 7:11–15*

**Jairus' daughter**
*Luke 8:41–42, 49–55*

**Lazarus**
*John 11:1–44*

**Dorcas**
*Acts 9:36–42*

**Eutychus**
*Acts 20:9–10*

# Parables and Illustrations of Jesus

## About nature and farm life

| | Matthew | Mark | Luke | John |
|---|---|---|---|---|
| Birds and flowers | 6:25–34 | 12:22–31 | | |
| A tree and its fruit | 7:15–20 | | 6:43–45 | |
| The sower | 13:1–9, 18–23 | 4:1–9, 13–20 | 8:4–8, 11–15 | |
| Growing seed | | 4:26–29 | | |
| Unfruitful fig tree | | | 13:6–9 | |
| Weeds | 13:24–30, 36–43 | | | |
| Mustard seed | 13:31–32 | 4:30–32 | 13:18,19 | |
| Lost sheep | 18:10–14 | | 15:1–7 | |
| Workers in the vineyard | 20:1–16 | | | |
| Tenants in the vineyard | 21:33–46 | 12:1–12 | 20:9–19 | |
| Fig tree | 24:32–35 | 13:28–31 | 21:29–33 | |
| Sheep and goats | 25:31–46 | | | |
| Harvest time | | | 4:35–38 | |
| The shepherd | | | 10:1–18 | |
| Grain of wheat | | | 12:20–26 | |
| The vine | | | 15:1–17 | |

## About Familiar Things in Bible Times

| | Matthew | Mark | Luke | John |
|---|---|---|---|---|
| Water | | | | 4:5–14; 7:37–39 |
| Salt | 5:13 | | | |
| Light | 5:14–16 | 4:21, 22 | 8:16–18 | 12:35–36 |
| Bread | | | | 6:25–35 |
| House builders | 7:24–27 | | 6:46–49 | |
| Patching clothes | 9:16 | 2:21 | 5:36 | |
| New wine | 9:17 | 2:22 | 5:37–39 | |
| Yeast | 13:33 | | 13:20–21 | |
| The pearl | 13:45–46 | | | |
| The fishing net | 13:47–50 | | | |
| Lost coin | | | 15:8–10 | |

## About Everyday Life

| | Matthew | Mark | Luke | John |
|---|---|---|---|---|
| Unwilling children | 11:16–19 | | 7:31–35 | |
| New truths and old | 13:51–52 | | | |
| Forgiveness | 18:21–35 | | | |
| Two sons | 21:28–32 | | | |
| The wedding feast | 22:1–14 | | 14:15–24 | |
| Ten girls at a wedding | 25:1–13 | | | |
| Servants | 25:14–30 | | 19:11–27 | |
| Debts and debtors | | | 7:41–47 | |
| Good Samaritan | | | 10:25–37 | |
| Friend in need | | | 11:5–13 | |
| Rich fool | | | 12:16–21 | |
| Watchful servants | | 13:33–37 | 12:35–40 | |
| Humility and hospitality | | | 14:7–14 | |
| Cost of discipleship | | | 14:25–33 | |
| Lost son | | | 15:11–32 | |
| Shrewd manager | | | 16:1–13 | |
| Rich man and Lazarus | | | 16:19–31 | |
| A servant's duty | | | 17:7–10 | |
| The persistent widow | | | 18:1–8 | |
| Pharisee and tax-collector | | | 18:9–14 | |

# Parables

Parables are stories based on everyday life. They teach a particular truth.
There are different types of parables:

- **short sayings,** for example "You are the light of the world" *Matthew 5:14a.*
- **longer sayings,** for example "No one sews a patch of unshrunk cloth on an old garment. If he does, the new piece will pull away from the old, making the tear worse" *Mark 2:21.*
- **complete stories,** for example the man sowing corn *Luke 8:4–8.*

Jesus' parables divided the listeners into two groups: those who wanted to understand and those who were unwilling or uninterested. To those who wanted understanding they were a means of learning more.

John never speaks about parables but he does use common things and everyday life to point to truths about God and God's world.

Jesus met the Samaritan woman at the well.

# Jesus' Last Week

## Jesus' Last Week

| | Matthew | Mark | Luke | John |
|---|---|---|---|---|
| **Sunday (Palm Sunday)** | | | | |
| Jesus enters Jerusalem in triumph | 21:1–9 | 11:1–10 | 19:28–44 | 12:12–19 |
| Jesus visits temple and returns to Bethany | 21:10–17 | 11:11 | 19:45–46 | |
| | | | | |
| **Monday** | | | | |
| Jesus curses an unfruitful fig tree | 21:18–19 | 11:12–14 | | |
| Jesus cleanses the temple court | | 11:15–19 | 19:45–48 | |
| | | | | |
| **Tuesday** | | | | |
| Jesus explains the withered fig tree | 21:20–22 | 11:20–26 | | |
| Jesus' authority is questioned | 21:23–27 | 11:27–33 | 20:1–8 | |
| Jesus teaches in the temple | 21:28–22:45 | 12:1–37 | 20:9–44 | |
| Jesus condemns the scribes and Pharisees | 23:1–36 | 12:37–40 | 20:45–47 | |
| Jesus points out the widow's gift | | 12:41–44 | 21:1–4 | |
| Jesus predicts the destruction of the temple and the end of the world | 24:1–44 | 13:1–37 | 21:5–36 | |
| | | | | |
| **Wednesday** | | | | |
| Jewish leaders conspire against Jesus | 26:1–5 | 14:1–2 | 22:1–2 | |
| Jesus anointed at Bethany | 26:6–13 | 14:3–9 | | |
| Judas agrees to betray Jesus | 26:14–16 | 14:10–11 | 22:3–6 | |
| | | | | |
| **Thursday (Maundy Thursday)** | | | | |
| Jesus prepares to celebrate Passover | 26:17–19 | 14:12–16 | 22:7–13 | |
| The Last Supper | 26:20–29 | 14:17–25 | 22:14–38 | 13:1–38 |
| Jesus and disciples withdraw to Gethsemane | 26:30–46 | 14:26–42 | 22:39–46 | 18:1 |
| Jesus betrayed and arrested | 26:47–56 | 14:43–52 | 22:47–53 | 18:2–12 |
| Jesus tried before Annas | | | | 18:12–14, 19–23 |
| Jesus before Caiaphas and the Sanhedrin; Peter's denial | 26:57–75 | 14:53–72 | 22:54–71 | 18:15–18, 24–27 |
| | | | | |
| **Friday (Good Friday)** | | | | |
| Jesus tried before Pilate; Judas's suicide | 27:1–10 | 15:1–5 | 23:1–5 | 18:28–38 |
| Jesus sent to Herod | | | 23:6–16 | |
| Pilate imposes sentence of death | 27:15–26 | 15:6–15 | 23:17–25 | 18:39–19:16 |
| Jesus scourged and led to Golgotha | 27:27–32 | 15:15–21 | | 19:16, 17 |
| Jesus' crucifixion and death | 27:33–56 | 15:22–41 | 23:33–49 | 19:18–30 |
| Jesus is buried | 27:57–61 | 15:42–47 | 23:50–56 | 19:31–42 |
| | | | | |
| **Saturday** | | | | |
| The tomb is guarded | 27:62–66 | | | |
| | | | | |
| **Sunday (Easter)** | | | | |
| The empty tomb and the risen Christ | 28:1–20 | 16:1–8 | 24:1–53 | 20:1–21:25 |

## What were Jesus' seven last sayings on the cross?

1. "Father, forgive them, for they do not know what they are doing." *Luke 23:34*
2. (To Mary) "Dear woman, here is your son." (To John) "Here is your mother." *John 19:26–27*
3. (To the criminal on the cross) "I tell you the truth, today you will be with me in paradise." *Luke 23:43*
4. "I am thirsty." *John 19:28*
5. "My God, my God, why have you forsaken me?" *Matthew 27:46; see Psalm 22:1*
6. "It is finished." *John 19:30*
7. "Father, into your hands I commit my spirit." *Luke 23:46*

## To whom did the risen Jesus appear?

1. **To Mary Magdalene at the tomb**
*Mark 16:9–11; John 20:11–18*
2. **To Mary Magdalene and "the other Mary"**
*Matthew 28:9–10*
3. **To Peter**
*Luke 24:34; 1 Corinthians 15:5*
4. **To the disciples on the road to Emmaus**
*Mark 16:12–13; Luke 24:13–35*
5. **To the apostles in the Upper Room when Thomas was absent**
*Mark 16:14–18; Luke 24:36–49; John 20:19–23*
6. **To the apostles in the Upper Room with Thomas present**
*John 20:24–29; 1 Corinthians 15:5*
7. **To the disciples at the Sea of Galilee**
*John 21:1–22*
8. **To the apostles on "the hill in Galilee"**
*Matthew 28:16–20; Mark 16:14*
9. **On the Mount of Olives**
*Luke 24:50–51; Acts 1:6–11*
10. **To more than 500**
*1 Corinthians 15:6*
11. **To James**
*1 Corinthians 15:7*
12. **To the apostles**
*Mark 16:9; Luke 24:44–52; Acts 1:4–9; 1 Corinthians 15:7*
13. **Many times in the 40 days after his resurrection**
*Acts 1:3*
14. **To Paul on the Damascus road**
*Acts 9; 22:6–10; 26:12–18; 1 Corinthians 15:8*

## The *I Ams* of John's Gospel

I am the bread of life 6:35–48
I am the living bread 6:51
I am the light of the world 8:12
I am from above; I am not of this world 8:23
I am the gate for the sheep 10:7
I am the good shepherd 10:11
I am the resurrection and the life 11:25
I am the way, and the truth and the life 14:6
I am the true vine 15:1

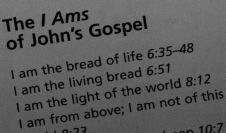

## What events will occur before Jesus' second coming?

- **Apostasy** *Matthew 24:10*
- **The rise of Antichrist** *Matthew 24:5, 23, 26*
- **Betrayal** *Mark 13:12; Luke 21:16*
- **Earthquakes** *Matthew 24:7; Mark 13:8*
- **False Christs** *Matthew 24:24; Mark 13:6, 21–23*
- **False prophets** *Matthew 24:11, 24; Mark 13:21–23*
- **False signs and miracles** *Matthew 24:24; Mark 13:22*
- **Famines** *Matthew 24:7*
- **Increase of evil** *Matthew 24:12*
- **International strife** *Matthew 24:7*
- **Persecution of believers** *Matthew 24:9; Mark 13:9–13*
- **Pestilence** *Luke 21:11*
- **Unparalleled distress** *Mark 13:17–19*
- **Wars and rumors of wars** *Matthew 24:6; Mark 13:7*
- **Worldwide proclamation of the Gospel** *Matthew 24:14; Mark 13:10*

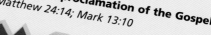

# Paul and the Early Churches

## What are the important dates and events in Paul's life?

| Approx. date | Events in Paul's Life | Roman History | Bible Reference |
|---|---|---|---|
| ?5 | Born in Tarsus | | |
| 14–37 | | Tiberius emperor | |
| 28–30 | Public ministry of Jesus | | *Luke 3:23* |
| 30 | Death of Jesus | | *Mark 15:37* |
| 33 | Converted on Damascus road | | *Acts 9:1–19* |
| 35 | First post-conversion visit to Jerusalem | | *Acts 9:26–30; Galatians 1:18* |
| 35–46 | In Cilicia (Tarsus) and Syria | | *Acts 11:25; Galatians 1:21* |
| 35–38 | Ministers in Arabia and Damascus | | *Galatians 1:17* |
| 37–41 | | Gaius emperor | |
| 41–54 | | Claudius emperor | |
| 43–46 | Ministers in Antioch with Barnabas | | *Acts 11:26* |
| 46 | Second (famine) visit to Jerusalem | | *Acts 11:30* |
| 47–49 | **First missionary journey** | | |
| | With Barnabas in Cyprus and Galatia | | *Acts 13:4–14:28* |
| | John Mark returns home from Perga | | *Acts 13:13* |
| 49 | Jerusalem Council | Jews expelled from Rome | *Acts 15:1–29* |
| 49–50 | *Letter to the Galatians* | | |
| 49–50 | **Second missionary journey** With Silas travels from Syrian Antioch through Asia Minor to Macedonia and Achaia Timothy joins them in Derbe Luke joins them in Troas? | | *Acts 15:36–18:22* *Acts 16:1* *Acts 16:8–9* |
| 50–52 | In Corinth | | *Acts 18:11* |
| 50 | *Letters to the Thessalonians* | | |
| autumn 51 | Leaves Corinth | | *Acts 18:18* |
| 51–52 | | Gallio proconsul of Achaia | |
| summer 52 | Third visit to Jerusalem | | |
| 52–59 | | Felix procurator of Judea | |
| 52–55 | **Third missionary journey** | | *Acts 18:23–21:17* |
| | In Ephesus | | *Acts 19:1–20:1* |
| 52–55 | *Letters to the Corinthians* | | |
| 54–68 | | Nero emperor | |
| 55–57 | In Macedonia, Illyricum, and Achaia | | *Acts 20:1–2* |
| winter 56/57 | In Corinth | | *Acts 20:3; 1 Corinthians 16:6* |
| | *Letter to the Romans* | | |
| May 57 | Fourth and last visit to Jerusalem | | *Acts 21:17–23:31* |
| 57–59 | Imprisoned and tried in Caesarea | | *Acts 23:31–26:32* |
| 59 | | Festus procurator of Judea | |
| September 59 | **Begins voyage to Rome** | | *Acts 25:10, 12; 27:1, 2* |
| February 60 | Arrives in Rome | | *Acts 28:14* |
| 60–62 | Under house arrest in Rome | | *Acts 28:30* |
| 62 | | Albinus procurator of Judea | |
| ?60–62 | *Prison Letters: Ephesians,* | | |
| 62 | *Philippians, Colossians, Philemon* | | |
| | Released from prison | | *Philippians 1:25* |
| 62–64 | Final ministry in the east? | | |
| July 64 | | Fire of Rome | |
| ?65 | Visits Spain? | | |
| ? | *Pastoral Letters: 1 & 2 Timothy, Titus* | | |
| ?67 | Re-imprisoned in Rome and executed | | |

# Which are the seven churches of Revelation?

**Ephesus** *Revelation 2:1–7*
Ephesus, an ancient city with a population of up to 500,000 situated on a major trade route, was the leading port of Asia Minor in New Testament times. It was created a free city in 98 BC, and its people, the Ephesians, were Roman citizens. The city was famed for the worship of Diana (Artemis), whose priestesses acted as cult prostitutes. Ephesus was also a center of the emperor cult, and a temple was built for the Emperor Domitian. The great theater of Ephesus, the remains of which still stand, held as many as 25,000 people.

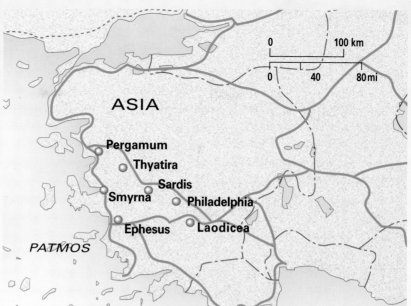

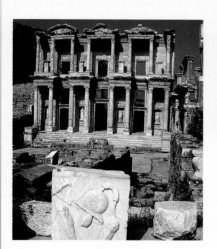

The reconstructed Library of Celsus, Ephesus.

The Roman forum Smyrna, modern Izmir.

**Smyrna** *Revelation 2:8–11*
Smyrna—modern Izmir—was a harbor with a population of around 200,000 in New Testament times. The city was famed for its "street of gold" with a temple at each end, and also boasted a wealthy academic community.

Remains of the Asclepium, Pergamum.

**Pergamum** *Revelation 2:12–17*
Pergamum, the capital of the Attalid kingdom during the 3rd–2nd century BC, housed the second largest library in the Roman Empire, and was also renowned for its parchment. The city was home to the Asclepion where a healing cult was practiced, and also housed a great altar of Zeus and three temples to the Roman emperor cult.

**Thyatira** *Revelation 2:18–29*
Thyatira—modern Akhisar—was located on an imperial post road, and had a great variety of trade guilds.

**Sardis** *Revelation 3:1–6*
Sardis was destroyed by a great earthquake in AD 17, and subsequently rebuilt by the Emperor Tiberius. It was a wealthy fortress city set on a hill, and was easily accessible from Asia Minor's most fertile river basin.

Remains of the Temple of Artemis, Sardis.

**Philadelphia** *Revelation 3:7–13*
Like Sardis, Philadelphia—modern Alasehir—was destroyed by the major earthquake of AD 17 and rebuilt by Tiberius. A fortress city on an imperial post road, Philadelphia was a significant Hellenistic educational center.

Ruins of ancient Laodicea.

**Laodicea** *Revelation 3:14–22*
Laodicea—modern Eski Hisar—suffered two earthquakes during the New Testament period, and was rebuilt once without imperial aid. World-famous as the producer of black wool, the city was also a center for banking and boasted an important medical school.

# Bible Names and People

## What are the titles of Jesus in the Bible?

**The beginning and the end** (Greek *Alpha* and *Omega*) *Revelation 1:8*

**Anointed One** *Psalm 2:2*

**Author of life** *Acts 3:15*

**Branch** *Zechariah 6:12*

**Bread of life** *John 6:35*

**Bright Morning Star** *Revelation 22:16*

**Christ** (Greek "Anointed One," or Messiah) *Matthew 16:16*

**Daystar** *2 Peter 1:19*

**Everlasting Father** *Isaiah 9:6*

**Gate** *John 10:7*

**Good shepherd** *John 10:11*

**Holy and Righteous One** *Acts 3:14*

**Holy One of God** *Mark 1:24*

**I am** *John 8:58*

**Immanuel** *Isaiah 7:14*

**Jesus** (Hebrew, "Yahweh saves") *Matthew 1:21*

**King of kings** *Revelation 17:14*

**Lamb** *Revelation 5:6–14*

**Lamb of God** *John 1:29*

**Last Adam** *1 Corinthians 15:45*

**Light of the world** *John 8:12*

**Lion of Judah** *Revelation 5:5*

**Lord** (Greek *Kyrios*) *Philippians 2:9–11*

**Lord of lords** *Revelation 17:14*

**Man of sorrows** *Isaiah 53:3*

**Master** *Luke 5:5*

**Messiah** (Hebrew for the "Anointed One") *John 1:41*

**Mighty God** *Isaiah 9:6*

**Nazarene** *Matthew 2:23*

**Prince of Peace** *Isaiah 9:6*

**Prophet** *Acts 3:22*

**Rabbi** *John 1:38*

**Resurrection and life** *John 11:25*

**Root of David** *Revelation 5:5*

**Root of Jesse** *Isaiah 11:10*

**Savior** *Luke 2:11*

**Son of David** *Matthew 1:1*

**Son of God** *Mark 1:1*

**Son of Man** *Matthew 8:20*

**True vine** *John 15:1*

**Way, truth, and life** *John 14:6*

**Wonderful Counselor** *Isaiah 9:6*

**Word** (Greek *Logos*) *John 1:1*

**Word of God** *Revelation 19:13*

## What are some of the names for the Holy Spirit in the Bible?

**Counselor** *John 14:16*

**Eternal Spirit** *Hebrews 9:14*

**Holy Spirit** *Luke 11:13*

**Power of the Most High** *Luke 1:35*

**Spirit** *Romans 8:26–27*

**Spirit of Christ** *Romans 8:9*

**Spirit of his [God's] Son** *Galatians 4:6*

**Spirit of holiness** *Romans 1:4*

**Spirit of the Lord** *Judges 3:10*

**Spirit of sonship** *Romans 8:15*

**Spirit of truth** *John 14:17*

## How is the church described in the Bible?

**Believers** *Acts 2:44*

**Body of Christ** *1 Corinthians 12:27*

**Bride** *Revelation 21:2*

**Called** *Romans 8:30; 1 Corinthians 1:2*

**Children of light** *Ephesians 5:8*

**Chosen people** *1 Peter 2:9*

**Christians** *Acts 11:26*

**Church** *Matthew 16:18; 18:17; 1 Corinthians 1:2*

**Citizens of heaven** *Philippians 3:20*

**Disciples** *Acts 6:1; 11:26*

**God's building; God's field** *1 Corinthians 3:9*

**God's children** *John 1:12; Romans 8:14–23*

**God's elect** *1 Peter 1:1*

**God's fellow-workers** *1 Corinthians 3:9*

**God's household** *Ephesians 2:19*

**God's temple** *1 Corinthians 3:16*

**Heirs of God** *Romans 8:17*

**Holy City** *Revelation 21:10–27*

**Holy nation** *1 Peter 2:9*

**Israel of God** *Galatians 6:16*

**Light of the world** *Matthew 5:14*

**Living stones** *1 Peter 2:5*

**People belonging to God** *1 Peter 2:9*

**Pillar and foundation of the truth** *1 Timothy 3:15*

**Royal priesthood** *1 Peter 2:9*

**Saints** *Ephesians 1:1, 15, 18; 3:18*

**Salt of the earth** *Matthew 5:13*

**Sanctified** *1 Corinthians 1:2*

**Sheep** *John 10:3*

**Soldiers of Christ** *2 Timothy 2:3–4*

**Strangers in the world** *1 Peter 1:1*

# Which Bible people saw God?

• Jacob dreamt of 'a stairway resting on the earth, with its top reaching to heaven, and the angels of God . . . ascending and descending'. *Genesis 28:12-13*

• 'Moses and Aaron, Nadab and Abihu, and the seventy elders of Israel went up and saw the God of Israel.' *Exodus 24:9-10*

• Moses saw the back of God. *Exodus 33:23*

• Micaiah saw 'the LORD sitting on his throne with all the host of heaven standing on his right and on his left'. *2 Chronicles 18:18*

• Isaiah saw 'the Lord seated on a throne, high and exalted'. *Isaiah 6:1*

• Ezekiel saw 'what looked like a throne of sapphire, and high above on the throne . . . a figure like that of a man'. *Ezekiel 1:26*

• Daniel saw thrones 'set in place, and the Ancient of Days took his seat. His clothing was as white as snow; the hair of his head was white like wool. His throne was flaming with fire.' *Daniel 7:9*

• Stephen looked up to heaven 'and saw the glory of God, and Jesus standing at the right hand of God'. *Acts 7:55*

• Paul wrote, 'I know a man in Christ who . . . was caught up to the third heaven.' *2 Corinthians 12:2*

• John wrote, 'I was in the Spirit, and there before me was a throne in heaven with someone sitting on it.' *Revelation 4:2*

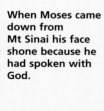

**When Moses came down from Mt Sinai his face shone because he had spoken with God.**

# What are the names and titles of God in the Bible?

**Ancient of Days** (Aramaic *Attiq yomin*) *Daniel 7:9* The ultimate authority as judge of the world.

**Creator** *Isaiah 40:28*

**Eternal God** (Hebrew *El Olam*) *Genesis 21:33*

**Father** (Greek *Theos ho Pater*) *Malachi 2:10; Matthew 6:9; Ephesians 3:14*

**Father of the heavenly lights** *James 1:17*

**God of Mountains** (Hebrew *El Shaddai*) *Genesis 17:1; 49:25* God is all-powerful.

**Most High** (Hebrew *El Elyon*) *Genesis 14:18-20* God, the maker of heaven and earth.

**God of all mankind** *Jeremiah 32:27*

**God of the covenant** (Hebrew *El Berit*) *Judges 9:46* Maker and keeper of his covenants.

**God of heaven** *Nehemiah 2:4*

**God of Israel** (Hebrew *El Elohe-Yisra'el*) *Genesis 33:20*

**Heavenly Father** *Matthew 6:26*

**Holy One** *Job 6:10*

**Holy One of Israel** (Hebrew *Qedosh Yisra'el*) *Isaiah 1:4*

**I AM** *Exodus 3:14*

**Judge** (Hebrew *Shapat*) *Genesis 18:25*

**King** *Jeremiah 10:7*

**King of kings** *1 Timothy 6:15*

**Living God** *Deuteronomy 5:26*

**LORD** (Hebrew *Yahweh*) *Exodus 3:13-16*

**God of Armies** (Hebrew *Yahweh-seba'ot, Sabaoth*) *1 Samuel 1:11; 17:45* God is all-powerful.

**LORD is my Banner** (Hebrew *Yahweh-nissi*) *Exodus 17:15* God gives us victories.

**LORD is Peace** (Hebrew *Yahweh-shalom*) *Judges 6:24* God brings us inner harmony.

**LORD is There** (Hebrew *Yahweh-shammah*) *Ezekiel 48:35* God will be with his people at the end of history.

**Lord of lords** *1 Timothy 6:15*

**Lord, Master** (Hebrew *Adonai*) *Psalm 2:4* God has authority.

**LORD Provides** (Hebrew *Yahweh-jireh*) *Genesis 22:14*

**LORD Our Righteousness** (Hebrew *Yahweh-tsidkenu*) *Jeremiah 23:6* By God's acts he declares and makes his people righteous.

**Saviour** (Greek *Soter*) *John 4:42*

**Word, The** (Greek *Logos*) *John 1:1* Jesus communicates God to humanity.

# Some Bible names and their meanings

**Aaron** *enlightened*
**Abel** *breath, a meadow*
**Abigail** *father of joy, father's joy*
**Abraham** *father of a multitude*
**Absalom** *father of friendship, or of peace*
**Adam** *human*
**Agrippa** *causing pain at birth*
**Ahaz** *possessor*
**Amos** *burden, one with a burden*
**Andrew** *a man, manly*
**Anna** *grace, gracious*
**Apollos** *belonging to Apollo*
**Aquila** *an eagle*

**Balaam** *foreigner, Lord of the people*
**Barnabas** *son of consolation*
**Bartholomew** *son of Ptolemy*
**Bathsheba** *daughter of an oath, or of seven*
**Benjamin** *son of the right hand*
**Bernice** *bringer of victory*
**Boaz** *fleetness, strength*

**Cain** *acquisition, possession*
**Caleb** *a barker, dog*
**Cephas** *stone, rock*
**Cornelius** *of a horn*
**Cyrus** *sun, splendour*

**Dan** *judge*
**Daniel** *God is my judge*
**David** *dear, beloved*
**Deborah** *bee*
**Delilah** *weak, tender, unhappy*

**Ehud** *the only*
**Eleazar** *God my helper*
**Eli** *lifting up*
**Elijah** *Yahweh my God*
**Elisabeth** *oath of God*
**Elisha** *God as a Saviour*
**Enoch** *dedicated, consecrated*
**Esau** *hairy*
**Esther** *star*
**Eve** *life, living*
**Ezekiel** *God will strengthen*
**Ezra** *help*

**Felix** *happy*
**Festus** *joyful*

**Gabriel** *man of God*
**Gad** *good fortune, fortunate*
**Gaius** *of the earth*
**Gideon** *a hewer, tree-feller*
**Goliath** *expulsion, expeller*

**Habakkuk** *embrace*
**Haggai** *festive*
**Ham** *hot, black*
**Hannah** *grace, prayer*
**Herod** *heroic*
**Hezekiah** *might of Yahweh*
**Hosea** *deliverance, salvation*

**Immanuel** *God with us*
**Isaac** *laughter*
**Isaiah** *salvation of Yahweh*
**Ishmael** *whom God hears*
**Israel** *soldier of God*

**Jacob** *supplanter*
**James** *supplanter*
**Jason** *healer*
**Jehoiakim** *set up by Yahweh*
**Jehoshaphat** *Yahweh judges*
**Jehovah** *(= Yahweh) the eternally existing*
**Jehu** *Yahweh is he*
**Jeremiah** *exalted by God*
**Jesse** *wealth*
**Jesus** *healer, saviour*
**Jethro** *pre-eminent*
**Jezebel** *chaste*
**Joab** *Yahweh is father*
**Job** *afflicted*
**Joel** *whose God is Yahweh*

Judas betrayed Jesus for 40 pieces of silver.

**John** *God's gift, grace*
**Jonah** *dove*
**Jonathan** *Yahweh is gracious*
**Joseph** *he shall add*
**Joshua** *Yahweh is salvation*
**Josiah** *God is healer*
**Jotham** *Yahweh is upright*
**Judah** *praised*
**Judas** *praised*
**Jude** *praised*
**Judith** *Jewess*

**Laban** *white, beautiful*
**Lazarus** *God my helper*
**Leah** *weary*
**Levi** *crowned*
**Lot** *covering, veil*
**Lucifer** *light-bringer*
**Luke** *light-giver*
**Lydia** *contention*

**Malachi** *messenger of Yahweh*
**Manasseh** *forgetting*
**Mark** *polite*
**Martha** *lady*
**Mary** *strong*
**Matthew** *gift of Yahweh*
**Melchizedek** *king of righteousness*
**Micah** *who is like God?*
**Miriam** *strong*
**Moab** *the desirable land*
**Mordecai** *consecrated to Merodach*
**Moses** *drawn out of the water*

**Nahum** *consolation, comforter*
**Naomi** *gracious, pleasant*
**Nathan** *gift (of God)*
**Nathanael** *gift of God*
**Nebuchadnezzar** *prince of the god Nebo*
**Nehemiah** *consolation from God*
**Nicodemus** *conqueror of the people*
**Noah** *rest*

**Obadiah** *servant of Yahweh*

**Paul** *little*
**Peter** *rock, stone*
**Philemon** *affectionate*
**Philip** *lover of horses*
**Priscilla** *ancient*

**Rachel** *ewe*
**Rahab** *gracious*
**Rebecca** *fetter*
**Reuben** *Yahweh has seen, God 's mercy*
**Ruth** *friend*

**Samson** *like the sun*
**Samuel** *name of God, placed by God, heard of God*
**Sarah** *princess*
**Saul** *asked for*
**Seth** *sprout*

Ruth would not desert her widowed mother-in-law.

**Simeon** *one heard*
**Simon** *one heard*
**Solomon** *peaceful*
**Stephen** *crown*

**Thaddaeus** *man of heart*
**Thomas** *twin*
**Timothy** *honoured by God*
**Titus** *honourable*

**Uriah** *light of Yahweh, Yahweh is my light*
**Uzziah** *power of Yahweh, strength of Yahweh*

**Zachariah** *remembered by Yahweh*
**Zedekiah** *justice of Yahweh*
**Zephaniah** *treasure of Yahweh*

Mary Magdalene, the first to see Jesus alive again.

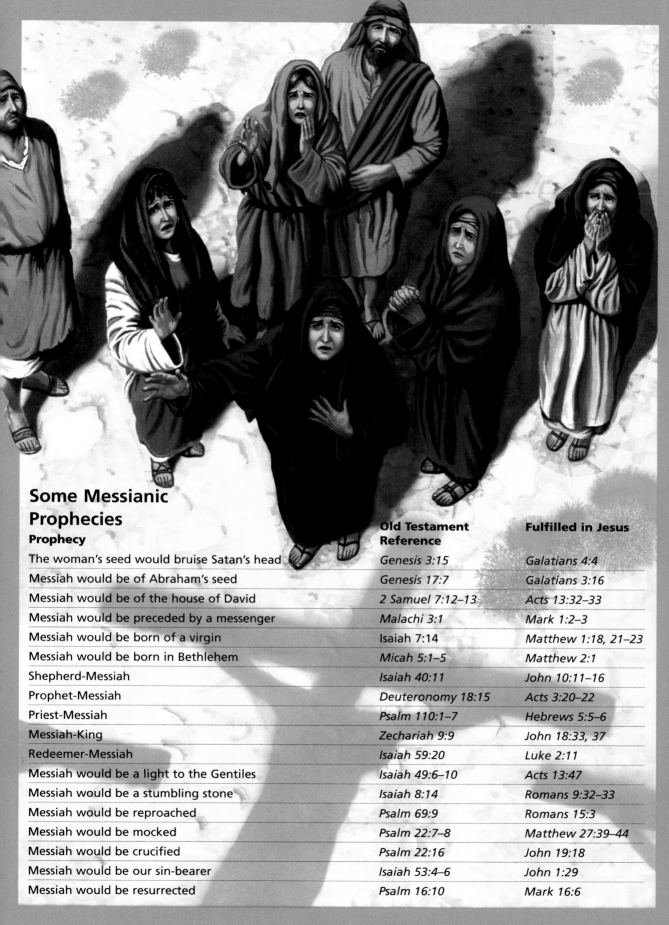

## Some Messianic Prophecies

| Prophecy | Old Testament Reference | Fulfilled in Jesus |
|---|---|---|
| The woman's seed would bruise Satan's head | Genesis 3:15 | Galatians 4:4 |
| Messiah would be of Abraham's seed | Genesis 17:7 | Galatians 3:16 |
| Messiah would be of the house of David | 2 Samuel 7:12–13 | Acts 13:32–33 |
| Messiah would be preceded by a messenger | Malachi 3:1 | Mark 1:2–3 |
| Messiah would be born of a virgin | Isaiah 7:14 | Matthew 1:18, 21–23 |
| Messiah would be born in Bethlehem | Micah 5:1–5 | Matthew 2:1 |
| Shepherd-Messiah | Isaiah 40:11 | John 10:11–16 |
| Prophet-Messiah | Deuteronomy 18:15 | Acts 3:20–22 |
| Priest-Messiah | Psalm 110:1–7 | Hebrews 5:5–6 |
| Messiah-King | Zechariah 9:9 | John 18:33, 37 |
| Redeemer-Messiah | Isaiah 59:20 | Luke 2:11 |
| Messiah would be a light to the Gentiles | Isaiah 49:6–10 | Acts 13:47 |
| Messiah would be a stumbling stone | Isaiah 8:14 | Romans 9:32–33 |
| Messiah would be reproached | Psalm 69:9 | Romans 15:3 |
| Messiah would be mocked | Psalm 22:7–8 | Matthew 27:39–44 |
| Messiah would be crucified | Psalm 22:16 | John 19:18 |
| Messiah would be our sin-bearer | Isaiah 53:4–6 | John 1:29 |
| Messiah would be resurrected | Psalm 16:10 | Mark 16:6 |

# Index

Copyright © 2001 Angus Hudson Ltd/Tim Dowley & Peter Wyart trading as Three's Company

Published in the United States by Kregel Publications, a division of Kregel Inc., P.O. Box 2607, Grand Rapids, Michigan 49501.

ISBN 0-8254-2452-6

All rights reserved. No part of this publication may be reproduced, stored in a retrieval system, or transmitted in any form or by any means – for example, electronic, photocopy, recording – without the prior written permission of the publisher. The only exceptions are brief quotations in printed reviews.

Designed by Peter Wyart, Three's Company

Worldwide co-edition organized and produced by Lion Hudson plc, Mayfield House, 256 Banbury Road, Oxford OX2 7DH, England.
Tel.: +44 1865 302750
Fax: +44 1865 302757
email: coed@lionhudson.com

Printed in Singapore

**Picture acknowledgments**
Photographs
Tim Dowley: pp. 5, 7, 8, 27
Israel Government Tourist Office: Sa'ar Ya'acov: p. 11
Peter Wyart: pp. 4, 12, 19, 27

Illustrations
Alan Harris: p. 13 bottom
James Macdonald: pp. 1, 4, 5, 6, 9, 13 top, 14, 16, 18 bottom, 19, 22, 25 left, 29 right
Kate Pascoe: pp. 17, 23
Richard Scott: pp. 8, 18 top, 21, 25 right, 29 left, 30, 31